The Trump Presidency

For Steven Poskanzer —
with thanks for your
support over the years.

Steve Schier
November 2017

The Trump Presidency

Outsider in the Oval Office

Steven E. Schier and Todd E. Eberly

ROWMAN & LITTLEFIELD
Lanham • Boulder • New York • London

Published by Rowman & Littlefield
A wholly owned subsidiary of The Rowman & Littlefield Publishing Group, Inc.
4501 Forbes Boulevard, Suite 200, Lanham, Maryland 20706
www.rowman.com

Unit A, Whitacre Mews, 26-34 Stannary Street, London SE11 4AB

British Library Cataloguing in Publication Information Available

Library of Congress Cataloging-in-Publication Data
Names: Schier, Steven E., author. | Eberly, Todd E., author.
Title: The Trump presidency : outsider in the oval office / Steven E. Schier
    and Todd E. Eberly.
Description: Lanham : Rowman & Littlefield, 2017. | Includes index.
Identifiers: LCCN 2017039928 (print) | LCCN 2017041612 (ebook) |
    ISBN 9781538105757 (electronic) | ISBN 9781538105733 (cloth : alk. paper) |
    ISBN 9781538105740 (pbk. : alk. paper)
Subjects: LCSH: Trump, Donald, 1946– | United States—Politics and
    government—2017–
Classification: LCC E913 (ebook) | LCC E913 .S35 2017 (print) |
    DDC 973.933092—dc23
LC record available at https://lccn.loc.gov/2017039928

♾™ The paper used in this publication meets the minimum requirements of American National Standard for Information Sciences—Permanence of Paper for Printed Library Materials, ANSI/NISO Z39.48-1992.

Printed in the United States of America

Contents

Preface

An Outsider in the Oval Office

No president has taken the oath of office with as little political experience as Donald Trump. The quintessential "outsider" candidate, he boasted a long career as a celebrity billionaire who exhibited brash language and behavior. Trump had never run for or held elective office or served in government before. Heavy (and often positive) media coverage during the 2016 primary campaign helped him capture the Republican presidential nomination, to the surprise of political "insiders" everywhere. In our first chapter we note that Trump's outsider movement, however, was hardly unprecedented in recent decades. Other insurgencies led by Ross Perot in the 1990s and the Tea Party and Occupy Wall Street in recent years challenged the political establishment before Trump.

The year 2016, however, proved to be a uniquely promising moment for an outsider like Trump to challenge established political elites of both parties. An overabundance of GOP presidential candidates—17 at the outset—helped Trump prevail with plurality victories in crucial early contests. Candidate Trump decided to self-fund, to bypass the traditional media approach, and to use whatever tactics kept his name in the headlines. His general election opponent was an "insider" seemingly sent from central casting—former secretary of state, New York senator, and first lady Hillary Rodham Clinton. In the campaign against Clinton, he rejected the traditional pivot to the center. Trump, the billionaire, managed to become the choice of working-class voters by channeling their anger and resentment toward the system. Voters wanted an outsider in the Oval Office, and that was never going to be Clinton.

Trump's flaws as a candidate, we note, caused him to underperform against Clinton in the November balloting. However, his appeal to aggrieved white working-class voters allowed him to narrowly carry the crucial Midwest industrial states of Wisconsin, Michigan, Ohio, and Pennsylvania, securing an Electoral College victory despite losing the popular vote by more than 2 percent. The postelection controversies involving state recounts and appeals to electors to change their votes reflected the highly polarized environment in which Trump, the provocative outsider, would take office.

Trump's initial months of navigating the institutional presidency revealed the steep learning curve an outsider encounters upon entering the Oval Office. Trump's personality, profiled in chapter 2, is that of a "dominator"—like Lyndon Johnson, Richard Nixon, and Andrew Jackson—whose temper and unpredictability foretells a stormy presidency. Trump's frequent verbal fusillades, erupting via his Twitter account and extemporaneous remarks to reporters, have produced a steady stream of controversies. We note how the pace of administration appointments initially lagged far behind that of his presidential predecessors and how his White House staff witnessed much turnover in a matter of mere months. Many of Trump's cabinet choices proved highly controversial and gained Senate approval by narrow party-line votes. One note of stability among the turbulence is his "team of generals" running the White House Office, National Security Council, and Defense Department, to whom Trump seems to pay heed. The role of family members—particularly daughter Ivanka and son-in-law Jared Kushner—have raised ethics questions, as have Trump's ties to Russia during the campaign and presidential transition that have received scrutiny by Special Counsel Robert Mueller.

In encountering Congress, President Trump discovered that governing as an outsider is far more challenging than campaigning as an outsider. That's our topic in chapter 3. Presidents have limited power and need to know how the system works (or at least hire people who know). But Trump didn't know and didn't trust folks from the inside. As a result, he alienated Congress almost from the beginning. Democrats, smarting from the election loss, have been in full attack mode throughout his presidency. Trump has had rocky relations with his own party in Congress, the Republicans who control both chambers. His loose understanding and uneven involvement of health-care reform contributed to its failure in Congress. Though touting a big agenda, Trump has been unable to stay on message. He's acted in ways that highlight his lack of experience, from a botched initial travel ban to the "transgenders in the military" tweet that did not quickly result in an actual policy directive. He attacked his own attorney general, Senate veteran Jeff Sessions (R-AL), and picked a fight with Senate Majority Leader Mitch McConnell (R-KY) without realizing the effect it would have on other lawmakers' willingness to trust him.

Difficulties with Congress have stalled important parts of Trump's domestic policy agenda, as we cover in chapter 4. His plans for tax reform, infrastructure spending, a border wall with Mexico, immigration reform, and deficit reduction progressed little on Capitol Hill in the early months of his presidency. Trump has, however, successfully achieved congressional passage of many rollbacks of federal regulations. Through the use of the Congressional Review Act, Trump and the Republican Congress have rescinded more than 30 Obama administration regulations subject to possible reversal under the act. Prior to this time, the Congressional Review Act had been used only once since its enactment in 1996. Trump has also employed the unilateral tools of presidential proclamations, memoranda, and executive orders to reverse additional regulations under his direct authority. No doubt the Trump administration will continue to pursue additional regulatory rollbacks.

Trump entered the Oval Office with no foreign policy experience. His campaign theme of "America First" suggested a major redirection of foreign policy. His initial attempts at immigration restriction, however, encountered judicial opposition. He was slow to fill subcabinet appointments in the state and defense departments. His secretary of state, Rex Tillerson, adopted a low profile and signaled no major rerouting of foreign policy. The former generals on his foreign policy team—Defense Secretary James Mattis, Chief of Staff John Kelly, and National Security Advisor H. R. McMaster—have not promoted a foreign policy revolution. Though Trump has issued vehement rhetoric about ISIS, Iran, and North Korea, so far his foreign policy has been cautious in its departures from established routine. His major changes involve withdrawing from the Paris Climate Accord, withdrawing from the Trans-Pacific Partnership trade agreement, attempting to install a temporary immigration ban affecting six Muslim nations, and prosecuting the Syrian conflict against ISIS more aggressively. Trump's rhetoric at times diverges from his policies, and this has often been the case in foreign policy.

What does the future hold for President Trump? His job approval in polls is uniquely low compared to his predecessors at comparable points in their first terms. Can he rally the nation and become a majority-approval president? Or can we expect more of the same—low popularity and constant controversy fueled by a frequently hostile media? Might ethics concerns or the Russia investigation lead to eventual impeachment and removal from office? In our final chapter, we examine the prospects for each of these scenarios. His presidency has been marred by missed opportunities in Congress, some setbacks in the courts, low popularity, and ongoing personnel drama. Thus far he's raised a very important question: Can an outsider govern?

1

❖ ❖

Trump's Victory
and Media Strategy

@realDonaldTrump
In addition to winning the Electoral College in a landslide, I won the popular vote if you deduct the millions of people who voted illegally. (3:30 p.m., November 27, 2016)

@realDonaldTrump
The FAKE NEWS media (failing @nytimes, @NBCNews, @ABC, @CBS, @CNN) is not my enemy, it is the enemy of the American People! (4:48 p.m., February 17, 2017)

It was not supposed to happen. In fact, there was certainty that it would not happen. Donald Trump would not become the forty-fifth president of the United States. The *New York Times*'s election prognostication website, "The Upshot," placed the probability of a Hillary Clinton victory at 85 percent (Katz 2016). Not to be outdone, the Huffington Post's Election 2016 model pegged the probability of a Clinton victory at 98 percent on the morning of the election (Jackson and Hooper 2016). The high level of confidence was shared by Clinton's campaign staff. The *New York Times* reported that her campaign team "popped open champagne on the campaign plane" on Election Day, certain of victory that night (Chozick 2016). Perhaps more folks should have listened to election prognosticator Nate Silver, who warned just one week from Election Day that Donald

Trump had a path to victory and that Hillary Clinton's electoral advantage was weak (NateSilver538 2016c). Though Clinton enjoyed a consistent lead in the national polls, her position in the Electoral College was never secure. In September 2016, FiveThirtyEight's Harry Enten (2016) warned that "Clinton does not have a meaningful advantage in the Electoral College" when compared to Barack Obama in 2012. In fact, FiveThirtyEight determined that Clinton was in a worse position, as compared to Obama, in 11 out of 15 battleground states (Enten 2016).

Five days before the election, Silver offered further warnings that there were far more undecided voters in 2016 than in 2012 and those voters could produce significant last-minute shifts in the election outcome. Silver even suggested that Pennsylvania and Michigan presented "risks" for Clinton just 5 days before the election (NateSilver538 2016b). Ryan Grim, Washington Bureau chief for the Huffington Post, was having none of it. Grim accused Silver of "putting his thumb on the scale" in favor of Trump and of "making a mockery" of the election-forecasting industry (Grim 2016). In the end, Silver was proven correct, and Donald Trump pulled off the biggest presidential election upset in the United States since Harry Truman defeated Thomas Dewey in 1948. Late on election night Grim tweeted an apology to Silver and pledged that he would "stick to punditry" from then on.

How did Trump do it? How did a billionaire and reality TV star with no political experience and a campaign in a seeming state of constant chaos defeat one of the most experienced and well-known and well-funded political dynasties in America? (Actually, he dispatched two dynasties if we include his easy defeat of Jeb Bush in the GOP primary.) There are many theories and, one year on from the election, a growing mountain of data and research that can help to answer that question. Beyond understanding why or how Trump won comes the need to understand what it means for American politics moving forward. Was 2016 a transformational or realigning election, or was it the final gasp of white voters before demographic changes deliver a more progressive era? Could it be that 2016 provided a rather conventional and even predictable election outcome even as it featured an unconventional and unpredictable campaign?

WAVES OF POPULAR DISCONTENT

In recent decades there has been a clear collapse in confidence in government and recurrent populist uprisings in America. The Perot candidacy in

1992, the Republican "revolution" of 1994, the Democratic sweep in the 2006 midterms, and the election of Barack Obama in 2008 are great national examples. In many respects, the surprise election victory of Donald Trump (and the unexpected strength of Sen. Bernie Sanders in the Democratic primary) was yet another manifestation of these populist uprisings. Though few predicted that Donald Trump would win the presidential election, his victory was decades in the making, and the signs of a victory like his were there for years.

Whenever national difficulties mount, popular anger is often focused on professional governing elites (Schier and Eberly 2013). The populist uprisings evident in recent years, including 2016, are an established aspect of the current American political system—a system marked not by unpredictability but by an era of stability in which the elections of 1974, 1980, 1994, 2006, 2008, 2010, 2014, and 2016 (in which popular discontent led to major electoral shifts) are recurrent features of a larger electoral pattern. The increased frequency of these uprisings suggests that popular resentments have burgeoned in recent years. After six years of Republican rule in Washington, the voters swept the GOP from congressional control in 2006. The 2008 election produced a change in party control in the White House and expanded Democratic Party control. The Tea Party movement of 2009, begun in response to the expansive spending and regulatory policies of the Obama administration, brought the GOP back into control of the House of Representatives with the midterm election of 2010. The Occupy Wall Street movement emerged in late 2011 and quickly spread to major cities throughout the United States. Declining voter turnout accompanied President Obama's narrow 2012 election victory, but weak economic and wage growth contributed to low public esteem of government, and in 2014 the voters delivered the Senate as well as the House to the Republicans. In state elections, the years between 2008 and 2014 saw the Democrats' once-dominant position in American politics diminish significantly as waves of popular discontent washed them from office. In recent years, popular distrust and discontent had risen to new and unprecedented highs.

The size and scope of what happened in November 2016 points, not necessarily to a realignment in American politics, but to a systemic reaction by the electorate. It was the manifestation of years, in fact decades, of rising levels of discontent by a growing number of disaffected voters. And into the midst of that discontent entered two immensely unpopular candidates for president. One, a former senator, a former secretary of state, a former candidate for president, the spouse of a former president, and the heir apparent to an outgoing two-term president, was the embodiment of the very political establishment that populist uprisings rail against. The other candidate . . . wasn't.

The populist uprising/popular discontent explanation for Trump's victory finds considerable support in election exit polls compiled by CNN ("Presidential" 2016). On Election Day 2016, fully 69 percent of voters were either dissatisfied with or angry at government, and Donald Trump won 58 percent of them. A plurality of voters, 48 percent, wanted the next president to be more conservative than Barack Obama, and Trump won 83 percent of them. A clear plurality, 39 percent, said the quality that mattered most to them in a new president was that he/she can bring change. Trump won 83 percent of those voters as well. Fully half of all voters said government already does too much as opposed to too little, and Donald Trump won 73 percent of them. Though Trump may have been a flawed candidate, Hillary Clinton was too removed from the prevailing mood of the electorate.

Preferring "conservative" government or believing that "government does too much" are clear signs of a collapse in trust in government (Schier and Eberly 2013). Hillary Clinton ran essentially as the candidate of Barack Obama's third term. She was the establishment. Given her résumé, she had no choice but to be the establishment candidate. And in her campaign, she surrounded herself with the establishment. She wrapped herself in the cloak of the Obama agenda. She did all of this in a year when most voters did not want the establishment to win. On questions of honesty and likability, it is clear that neither candidate was liked, and most people were not happy with the choice presented them in 2016. In a rather telling finding, fully 60 percent of voters said Trump was not qualified to be president. Yet he still managed to win 20 percent of those folks. This was an election based on discontent and frustration, and little else mattered.

Though Clinton and her supporters have offered myriad explanations for her defeat—from Russian interference, WikiLeaks, the decision by former FBI director James Comey to reopen the investigation into Clinton's unsecured email server used while secretary of state, and misogyny—exit poll data suggests that Clinton lost for many of the same reasons that prior candidates have lost. Exit polls show that more than two-thirds of the electorate were either dissatisfied with or angry at the federal government, and Trump won those voters by 21 points. Nearly two-thirds of the electorate said that the American economy was in poor shape, and Trump won those voters by a two-to-one margin. Nearly two-thirds of the electorate said the country was headed in the wrong direction, and Trump carried them by nearly three-to-one. These results are very similar to the factors that led to John McCain's defeat against Barack Obama in 2008.

Beyond exit polls and popular discontent, history is also instructive as to the reasons for Trump's victory. It is extremely rare for voters to follow a two-term president by electing a candidate from that president's party. George H. W. Bush in 1988 is the only recent example. So Hillary Clinton suffered the same fate as most post-incumbent partisans, including Adlai Stevenson in 1952, Richard Nixon in 1960, Al Gore in 2000, and John McCain in 2008. It's no wonder, then, that election prediction models developed by economists and political scientists and based on so-called "fundamental" factors such as economic growth, consumer confidence, and incumbent approval rating painted a picture of the 2016 election outcome that was far less certain than those predictions based almost entirely on public opinion polls (Mann 2016).

In September 2016, results from 9 such models set to be featured in the journal *PS: Political Science and Politics* were released, and they revealed no consensus regarding who would win, let alone what the margin of victory would be. Tellingly, those models based more on historic fundamentals such as economic conditions or incumbent approval tended to see a rosier picture for Donald Trump. Models that relied more on contemporary public opinion polls painted a better picture for Hillary Clinton. All told, existing predictive models and a review of American presidential elections pointed to a very close election and one where the incumbent party would face disadvantages. But these *fundamentals* were often overshadowed by the larger-than-life major-party candidates vying for the presidency. Trump's lack of qualifications, unorthodox style, and frequent tendency to say or do offensive things compared poorly to Hillary Clinton's extensive résumé and measured tone. The stark contrast created the impression of an election outcome that was easier to predict.

It's difficult to estimate the effect, individually or combined, of the myriad factors that may have contributed to the outcome. There can be no doubt that Russian agents interfered in the election. Less clear is whether that interference substantively affected the outcome. It's clear that Russian hackers were successful in breaching the email servers of the Democratic National Committee as well as the email account of Clinton campaign chief John Podesta. They were effective as well at hyping the contents of hacked emails. But there's no evidence that the Russians breached any election systems or interfered with the actual vote (Sheth and Bertrand 2017). Though the steady drip of leaked emails may have contributed to voters' lack of trust in Clinton, there were serious missteps taken by the candidate and campaign as well. The FBI investigation into Clinton's use of a private and unsecured email server while secretary of state was a controversy of Clinton's own making. Bill Clinton's impromptu private meeting with Attorney General Loretta Lynch, in the midst of the investigation, when their planes crossed paths at a Phoenix airport certainly did not help, either (Watkins 2016). Though Hillary Clinton clearly believes that James Comey's decision to reopen the investigation into her email server just 10 days prior to the election was crucial to understanding her loss (Rucker 2017), a panel of polling experts convened to understand how pollsters got the election wrong concluded that the evidence of a Comey effect was "mixed" at best (Kurtzleben 2017). Another counterpoint to the Comey as cause conclusion is that Clinton's lead over Trump in the polls was already declining in the days before the Comey announcement (Cohn 2017). The decline began following a widely covered announcement of substantial premium increases under the Affordable Care Act (Luhby 2016).

But it's important to note that just because Trump's victory was unexpected it was not necessarily very impressive in a historical context. Trump was the weakest post-incumbent challenger in 200 years (McLaughlin 2017a). Including 2016 there have been a total of 17 presidential elections in which no incumbent was on the ballot following the reelection of an incumbent. In the prior 16 post-incumbent elections there was a very clear trend in both the popular (state and national) and the electoral vote, a significant shift of votes to the party that was out of power (McLaughlin 2017b). How significant a swing? Across the prior 16 post-incumbent elections, that average vote swing toward the party out of power was 10 percentage points. If the analysis is narrowed to only those post-incumbent elections to have occurred after the Civil War, the swing is 6 percentage points in the popular vote. Barack Obama won the popular vote by 3.9 percentage points, with 51.1 percent to Romney's 47.2 percent of the vote. In a hypothetical post-incumbent election in 2016, history would suggest that a 6-point shift would deliver 45.1 percent to the Democrat and 53.2 percent to the Republican. Hillary Clinton outperformed the historical pattern, receiving 48.2 percent of the vote, and Trump underperformed with 46.1 percent (McLaughlin 2017b). Trump also ran poorly compared to other Republicans on the ballot. Republican candidates for the House of Representatives won the popular vote by nearly 1.4 million votes, receiving 49.1 percent of the vote to Trump's 46.1 percent. Trump trailed the

Republican Senate candidates in most of the states with a contested race (McLaughlin 2017b).

Trump's underperformance relative to other post-incumbent challengers coupled with Clinton's overperformance suggests that Trump's flaws as a candidate were a drag on his campaign. Revelations in an *Access Hollywood* tape of Trump bragging that his star power allowed him to grope women and that he tried very hard to initiate an affair with a married woman almost certainly harmed his campaign and limited his ability to attract voters. Trump's frequent attacks on women's appearance and the multiple accusation that he had sexually harassed women were harmful as well. Trump won by winning 3 of the 4 states that were decided by less than 1 percentage point—Michigan, New Hampshire, Pennsylvania, and Wisconsin. A shift of 40,000 votes from Trump to Clinton in Michigan, Pennsylvania, and Wisconsin would have delivered the presidency to Clinton. The race was just that close for Clinton, and history suggests that it should not have been. With every presidential election there is a tendency among scholars and pundits to ask whether the outcome had resulted in a dramatic political reordering. There is reason to conclude that 2016 delivered a fairly conventional outcome, despite the presence of two historically unpopular candidates and one decidedly unconventional candidate.

Though some have suggested that the Libertarian candidate Gary Johnson and Green Party candidate Jill Stein may have cost Clinton the election, this is a rather specious claim. As a limited government Libertarian, it's reasonable to conclude that Johnson drew more votes from Trump than from Clinton. Jill Stein may have appealed to more progressive voters turned off by Clinton's connections to the establishment. In Michigan, Pennsylvania, and Wisconsin there were just enough Stein votes such that a reallocation of nearly every Stein vote to Clinton would have changed the outcome. But a study by political scientists Christopher Devine and Kyle Kopko raises serious doubts about the validity of simply reassigning Stein's voters to Clinton. Their analysis of exit polling data in those three key states determined that Stein's absence from the race may have delivered Michigan to Clinton, but not Wisconsin or Pennsylvania. Pennsylvania and Wisconsin would have been tied, with Clinton and Trump having a 50–50 chance of winning each. But even this analysis likely overstates Stein's impact, as it assumes that her supporters would've shown up on Election Day had she not been on the ballot (Devine and Kopko 2016).

TRUMP, THE PRESS, AND SOCIAL MEDIA

Nearly a year into his presidency, it may seem odd to suggest that Donald Trump owes much of the credit for his rise from reality TV star to president to the press. His first year in office has been marked by several high-profile disputes with the "mainstream media," or MSM, as it is often called. But it's hard to imagine a nominee Trump, let alone a President Trump, without giving some credit to frequent, and favorable, coverage that Trump received upon announcing his candidacy in the summer of 2015 and effectively securing the Republican nomination in May 2016. Political scientists refer to the months leading up to the first presidential primary or caucus as the invisible primary. It's a time period during which potential candidates compete to secure money, endorsements, staff commitments, and, perhaps most important, press coverage. Simply stated, media exposure can boost a candidate's standing in public opinion polls, and improved standing in polls can bolster a candidate's ability to secure endorsements and raise money. Trump was able to couple his traditional media coverage with an unprecedented use of social media to propel himself to the Republican nomination and then to the presidency.

Prior to the Trump candidacy, there was a conventional wisdom regarding the invisible primary. Essentially, it was argued that endorsements and money were key to early success. From that success a candidate could expect rising poll numbers, and with rising poll numbers would come more media coverage. Likewise, missteps and misstatements could derail a campaign before it ever truly began. The press is a crucial player during the invisible primary. Prior to reforming the nominating system in the early 1970s it was political party power brokers, party bosses, who played the role of filtering out candidates who were not quite ready for prime time and promoting those deemed worthy of consideration. Since the 1970s, however, that screening process has fallen mostly to the press (Patterson 2016d). Most voters learn about politics and candidates secondhand, via the news, so media coverage can be crucial to a candidate's success or failure. Additionally, the media has traditionally served as an arbiter of what a candidate can or cannot say without paying a political price. For decades, the acceptable bounds of public opinion have been viewed within the confines of Overton's window. Named for its creator, Joseph Overton, Overton's window defines the range of acceptable opinions that can be expressed by politicians. Trump did not simply test the boundaries of acceptable rhetoric; he also relied on an extensive social media following to redefine them (Ranzini 2016).

The following sampling of tweets was selected from those he posted as a candidate and those he posted as president. Each tweet is prefaced by a short description of the circumstances surrounding the tweet.

Donald Trump launched his presidential campaign with a brutal assessment of illegal immigration in America: "When Mexico sends its people, they're not sending their best. . . . They're sending people that have lots of problems, and they're bringing those problems with us. They're bringing drugs. They're bringing crime. They're rapists. And some, I assume, are good people" (Kopan 2016). Trump faced a tremendous backlash for the comments, but just one month later he refused to apologize.

@realDonaldTrump
Likewise, billions of dollars gets brought into Mexico through the border. We get the killers, drugs & crime, they get the money!
(6:53 a.m., July 13, 2015)

At the first Republican primary debate in August 2015, former Fox News anchor Megyn Kelly took Trump to task for his history of derogatory comments against women. In an interview following the debate, Trump said of Kelly, "She gets out and she starts asking me all sorts of ridiculous questions. . . . You could see there was blood coming out of her eyes, blood coming out of her wherever. In my opinion, she was off base" (Rucker 2015). Months later, Trump, by then the GOP front-runner, was still angry with Kelly's coverage of him when he tweeted:

@realDonaldTrump
I refuse to call Megyn Kelly a bimbo, because that would not be politically correct. Instead I will only call her a lightweight reporter!
(6:44 a.m., January 27, 2016)

As the battle for the GOP nomination began, there was an informal truce between Trump and Senator Ted Cruz, as Cruz refused to challenge Trump the way other candidates did. By February 2016, Cruz was rising in the polls and started becoming more critical of Trump. As Cruz began to rise, Trump pushed a theory that Cruz was ineligible for the the presidency because he wasn't a natural-born citizen as required by the US Constitution. Ted Cruz was born in Canada. His mother was a US citizen, but his father was Cuban. Under federal law, anyone born to a US citizen is a natural-born citizen. But Trump was pushing the notion that to be a natural-born citizen one must be born in the United States. His challenge of Cruz's citizenship was reminiscent of his past claims that Barack Obama was actually born in Kenya and was not eligible to be president.

@realDonaldTrump
If @TedCruz doesn't clean up his act, stop cheating, & doing negative ads, I have standing to sue him for not being a natural born citizen.
(2:45 p.m., February 12, 2016)

Trump's derogatory comments about Mexican immigrants continued to dog his campaign. Matters became worse in April 2016 when federal judge Gonzalo Curiel was presiding over a class-action lawsuit concerning students who said they were defrauded by Trump University. Trump publicly claimed that there was a conflict of interest and that Curiel would not be fair to Trump because of Curiel's "Mexican heritage" and Trump's plan to build a border wall between the United States and Mexico. Curiel was born in Indiana to parents who had legally emigrated to the United States from Mexico. In May, Trump decided that posing with a taco bowl purchased from the Trump Tower Grill would be a good way to smooth things over.

@realDonaldTrump
Happy #CincoDeMayo! The best taco bowls are made in Trump Tower Grill. I love Hispanics!
(2:57 p.m., May 5, 2016)

As president, Trump saw little reason to reconsider his unfiltered Twitter strategy. In late January 2017 Donald Trump issued a controversial executive order banning travel to the United States from seven majority Muslim nations. In early February a federal judge blocked the travel ban from going into effect. Trump made his displeasure with the judge very clear. Many observers were shocked by Trump's implication that the judge would bear personal responsibility for any attack that might happen while the ban is blocked.

@realDonaldTrump
Just cannot believe a judge would put our country in such peril. If something happens blame him and court system. People pouring in. Bad!
(3:39 p.m., February 5, 2017)

In the early morning of March 4, 2017, President Trump issued an accusation that President Obama had ordered the wiretapping of Trump Tower, the location of Trump's home as well as his campaign headquarters. Such an action by Obama would have been an explosive revelation. Yet Trump had no evidence to support the claim, and no evidence ever surfaced. Senior members of the intelligence community refuted the claims, and as president, Trump would have the authority to reveal whether any such wiretapping had been ordered or approved. No evidence to support the claim was ever found, but Trump never backed down from his allegation.

> @realDonaldTrump
> Terrible! Just found out that Obama had my "wires tapped" in Trump Tower just before the victory. Nothing found. This is McCarthyism!
> (6:35 a.m., March 4, 2017)

The national press, and his political opponents, routinely condemned Trump for his often-inflammatory comments and tweets. Rather than harm Trump's campaign, the increased coverage boosted his campaign. Research has shown a link between simple and informal rhetoric and campaign success and that candidates that can match the complexity of their message to the understanding of their audience tend to have greater success (Ahmadian, Azarshahi, and Paulhus 2017). Trump was able to use social media, especially Twitter, to connect with voters who held views on politics and policy matters that existed outside the defined parameters of Overton's window (Ranzini 2016). To the shock of many political observers, such voters existed in greater numbers than they had suspected.

During the 2015 invisible primary Donald Trump received far more media coverage than any of his Republican rivals, and the coverage that he received was overwhelmingly positive or neutral, a combination of coverage defined as favorable (Patterson 2016d). This coverage advantage appears to have violated two long-standing norms of invisible primary media coverage. One, poll standing tends to determine how much media coverage a candidate receives; and two, press coverage during this phase is typically focused on a candidate's fund-raising prowess. During the invisible primary, however, former Florida governor Jeb Bush was atop the polls and had raised far more money than any other potential Republican candidate. Donald Trump barely registered in the polls and had raised no money. Yet Trump received twice the amount of media coverage than did Bush (Patterson 2016d). This coverage translated into millions of dollars in free media exposure and most certainly bolstered his campaign and contributed to his steady rise in opinion polls. Beyond receiving more coverage than his potential rivals, Trump received more favorable coverage.

Thomas Patterson of the Shorenstein Center on Media, Politics and Public Policy explains that Trump benefited from the fact that journalists are attracted "to the new, the unusual, the sensational" (2016d, 5), and Trump was a perfect candidate to draw that attraction. Patterson declares Trump "arguably the first bona fide media-created presidential nominee" (5). *New York Times* columnist Nicholas Kristof echoed that sentiment, writing that "we in the news media gave Trump $1.9 billion in free publicity in this presidential cycle. That's 190 times as much as he paid for in advertising, and it's far more than any other candidate received" (2016). Neither Patterson's nor Kristof's observation negates the fact that Trump was able to tap into an underlying current of discontent and voter anger; rather, it suggests that without the media Trump's lack of a political constituency and credible claims to the presidency might have prevented him from making that connection with the electorate.

It may be hard to believe that most of Trump's media coverage was favorable during the crucial months of the invisible primary, but that largely resulted from the narratives typically employed by the press during the early stages of a campaign. Early coverage is mostly focused on the horse-race aspect of the campaign. A candidate's position in the horse race typically fits into one of four possible story lines: a candidate may be leading, gaining ground, losing ground, or trailing. As one might imagine, stories about candidates leading or gaining ground tend to be more favorable, as they focus on those things going well within the campaign. Likewise, stories about a candidate trailing or losing tend to be unfavorable, as the focus is often on those aspects of the campaign that are going wrong (Patterson 2016d). This horse-race approach to coverage benefited Trump and hurt Jeb Bush, the assumed front-runner. As a result of the free media coverage afforded Trump, his poll numbers began to rise. So stories written about the Trump candidacy often focused on his rise from a candidate with no real support to a real contender. Jeb Bush, however, found himself on the losing ground end of coverage, as stories focused on the failure of his endorsements, fund-raising, or poll position to secure the nomination. It's important to note that nearly all of the coverage of Trump during this stage focused on the horse race, and very little focused on his personal characteristics or policy issues (Patterson 2016d). As an aside, it merits mention that most of Hillary Clinton's invisible primary coverage was negative.

Trump's domination of media coverage continued throughout the primary season. Trump's string of primary victories and rising delegate count resulted in favorable coverage, still fixated on the horse race, until the very last month of the primary season and after all of his potential opponents had dropped out of the race. This was driven by the dynamic of Trump as the candidate gaining ground or leading. Perhaps more surprising, Trump continued to receive more media coverage than Clinton or Bernie Sanders even after the Republican nomination battle was essentially over. But the tone of the coverage changed. In the final month of primary contests, with all challengers vanquished, Trump's coverage went from 53–47 percent positive in the preceding months to 61–39 percent unfavorable in the closing weeks. Why the change? With the nomination all but secured, stories about the horse race became less common. More coverage focused on Trump's personality and his issue positions. Those horse-race stories that did appear tended to focus on him trailing Clinton or Sanders in the general election. In short, coverage of Trump did not turn negative until attention shifted away from the Republican primary horse race and to the 2016 general election (Patterson 2016c).

GEOGRAPHY TRUMPS DEMOGRAPHY

In 2002, John Judis and Ruy Teixeira wrote "The Emerging Democratic Majority." In it, they theorized that Democrats were on the verge of establishing a lock on the Electoral College. According to their argument, Democrats were strongest in the "post-industrial" sections of the country where the production of ideas had replaced manufacturing. Republicans were strongest in the regions where the transition to post-industrialism had lagged. Judis and Teixeira argued this new majority was driven by demographic changes taking place in growing metropolitan regions that would serve as the breeding ground of the new Democratic majority. The key to the emerging Democratic majority was demography. The key metropolitan regions were home to the growing minority and professional populations essential to Democrats. As argued by the authors, this emerging majority included another crucial member—the white working class. Though these former members of the Democratic coalition had abandoned the party for Ronald Reagan, they increasingly came to share the values of their professional counterparts. As such, "Republican appeals to race (or resentment against immigrants), guns, and abortion have largely fallen on deaf ears, and these voters have not only rejected Republican social conservatism, but also reverted to their prior preference for Democratic economics" (2002).

The 2006 midterm elections, followed by Barack Obama's comfortable victory in 2008, convinced many that the Democratic majority had indeed emerged (Klinkner and Schaller 2009). The substantial Republican victories in 2010, however, raised serious doubts about the demographics-as-destiny theory of the emerging Democratic majority. Following Barack Obama's comfortable reelection in 2012, Ruy Teixeira argued that the election result vindicated the arguments presented in the emerging Democratic majority and suggested that said majority might be here to stay (Teixeira 2012), but only if Democrats embraced and pursued the activist government progressive legacy of the 1960s. Then came 2014 and the culmination of the Republican gains made in Congress, statehouses, and state legislatures during Obama's tenure. Teixeira's coauthor, John Judis (2015), revisited the emerging majority thesis in 2015 and concluded that their theory was flawed, perhaps fatally. Not only had white working-class voters continued their decades-long migration to the Republican Party, but middle-class whites were also joining them in the journey. More troubling for the theory was the fact that middle-class Hispanics and young voters were less Democratic than had been predicted (Judis 2015).

In the 2016 election, Trump's victory revealed many of the flaws that Judis had identified in the emerging majority thesis. According to exit polls, Donald Trump won an overwhelming majority of white working-class voters (Desk, NBC News 2016). In the key battleground states (and central bricks in Clinton's "Blue Wall") of Pennsylvania, Ohio, Michigan, and Wisconsin, Trump saw the Republican margin of victory among white working-class voters grow from 12 points in 2012 to 30 points in 2016. But the emerging Democratic majority included more than just white working-class voters, and even among those other voting blocs Trump defied expectations. He carried college-educated whites as well as suburban voters, which Judis and Teixeira viewed as a crucial component of the emerging Democratic majority. Trump received the support of 61 percent of white working-class women and split the vote of married women with Clinton. Though he lost black and Hispanic women by wide margins, he did better among those groups against Clinton than had Mitt Romney against Obama in 2012. Trump performed better among Hispanic voters in general than had Mitt Romney. Among young voters, Clinton's 19-point advantage over Trump was decidedly smaller than Obama's 23-point advantage in 2012 or his 34-point advantage in 2008.

It's pretty clear that Judis and Teixeira overstated the potential for an emergent Democratic majority. But their error may go beyond misstating how key demographic groups would vote. Their reliance on demographics, in an electoral system driven more by geography, was likely an error as well. The emerging Democratic majority was very much premised on demographics as key Democratic constituencies grew in strength and number in major metropolitan areas. By their very numbers they would come to dominate American politics and elect Democrats. The flaw in the theory was laid bare in a multipart analysis conducted by Sean Trende and David Byler for the popular RealClearPolitics website (2017). Simply stated, if the Democrats' greatest strength is demographic, then the GOP's greatest strength is geographic. The Democratic Party's coalition is poorly distributed throughout the United States. It is overwhelmingly concentrated in large metropolitan regions, which limits the party's ability to win.

In 2016 Hillary Clinton won the largest metropolitan areas by a historic margin of 30 points, and that margin in highly populated areas certainly contributed to her 3-million-vote popular vote win. But these large metropolitan areas are mostly located in already Democratic, non-swing states. So her margins added to her popular vote total but not her electoral vote total. However, Clinton not only lost but also performed worse than any recent Democrat in small cities and towns and in rural America. In the swing states like Florida, there are more than enough votes in those areas to offset an advantage in the large metropolitan regions. In 2000, Al Gore won the popular vote by 550,000 votes and lost the election by an agonizingly close 4 electoral votes. Much like Clinton, Gore won in the largest metropolitan areas and lost in small cities and towns and in rural America. But the gap between his vote share in the largest metropolitan regions as compared to rural America was approximately 18 percentage points. Hillary Clinton won the popular vote by 3 million votes but lost the election by a decidedly not close 72 electoral votes. The gap between her support in large metropolitan areas and rural America was 32 percentage points (Trende and Byler 2017)!

In some respects, Clinton inherited a Democratic Party dominated by voters from increasingly progressive urban areas. As such, the party has tailored its message and policy agenda to maximize support from those areas but at the expense of a growing number of voters, especially white working-class and middle-class suburban voters. Equally as important as the flawed demographic assumptions made by Teixeira and Judis were their assumptions about support for activist government. On Election Day

2016 nearly 70 percent of voters said that they were dissatisfied or angry with the federal government, and by a 50–45 percent margin voters said that government is doing too much as opposed to too little ("Presidential" 2016). By a 3–1 margin voters wanted the next president to be more conservative than Barack Obama as opposed to more liberal. Both Donald Trump and Hillary Clinton were historically unpopular, and a majority of voters considered Trump unqualified for the presidency, but Trump was the candidate who better reflected voter attitudes regarding government. The concentrated nature of the Democratic coalition, and the tailoring of the party's message to progressive and urban voters, not only contributed to Trump's victory but also handicapped the Democrats in Senate and House races (Trende and Byler 2017).

FROM CANDIDATE TO PRESIDENT

There can be no question that Donald Trump ran an unorthodox campaign for the presidency. Throughout the campaign, observers and commentators often wondered if there would be a "pivot" at some point when Trump would become a more traditional candidate (Waldman 2016). Trump's style was simply too brash, too uncouth, too undisciplined, and at times too offensive and vulgar to be a winning strategy. But Trump became the GOP front-runner, and there was no pivot. He became the nominee with no pivot. And thus far he has been president with no pivot. Trump the president is every bit as brash, uncouth, undisciplined, and at times offensive and vulgar as he was as a candidate. When questioned on the seemingly unpresidential nature of his statements and social media musings, Trump declared (in a tweet, of course) that he was "MODERN DAY PRESIDENTIAL" (Wootson 2017).

Though Trump's bold claim may be debatable, what is not debatable is that Trump is president. Trump could be forgiven for questioning why he should adopt a new style or "pivot" given all that he has accomplished. It's certainly possible that Trump won in spite of his boorish behavior, but it's worth considering as well that he won in part because of it. Research has shown that voters tend to react positively to candidates who communicate in a more informal way. Compared to his Republican opponents and to Hillary Clinton, Donald Trump made more use of nonstandard and low-complexity words and made much greater use of Twitter (considered a less formal form of communication [Ahmadian et al. 2017; Sclafani 2017]).

According to linguist Jennifer Sclafani, who spent two years studying Trump, his communication style was crucial to his success, and he connected with many voters because he communicates the way that they do. Unlike most politicians or presidents, Trump does not speak in a manner that conveys a greater level of education or refinement than his audience. His tendency to use simple two- or three-word phrases, a casual tone, repetition, and hyperbole—even his frequent midsentence topic changes—reflect things that people do in everyday speech. Trump clearly recognized that he was connecting with voters when he remarked during a February 2017 news conference, "That's how I won . . . I won with news conference and probably speeches. I certainly didn't win by people listening to you people, that's for sure" (Inzaurralde 2017).

But clearly there were limits to his appeal. Though Trump won, he lost the popular vote by 3 million votes. As president, his approval rating has been mired in negative territory (Gallup 2017). His inflammatory rhetoric has added a new layer to America's already polarized politics. Offensive statements made about immigrants, women, members of Congress, judges, and others have created difficulty reaching out to members of his own party, let alone attempting to build bridges with Democrats. Congressional Democrats who may otherwise be open to working with Trump on matters such as infrastructure face the possibility of open revolt among the base of the party, the most active members of which have formed a "resistance" movement dedicated to blocking Trump and his agenda and declared the start of "Resistance Summer" in June 2017 (Ferrechio 2017). Even a majority of Republicans believe that Trump is undermining his agenda with his rhetoric (Blanton 2017). As is discussed in subsequent chapters, Trump's agenda is ambitious, and his Senate majority is slim; it may prove very difficult to achieve success as president by relying on the tactics that won him the presidency. But well into his first year in office Trump shows little willingness to pivot, and it's not altogether clear that those whom he has offended would be willing to consider a more traditionally presidential Donald Trump.

THE LAYOUT OF THE BOOK

The initial section of each of the chapters to follow will contain a factual summary of the Trump presidency's action in each area. The later theoretical sections of each chapter place the initial actions, successes and failures, challenges and growth within the larger context of the political system and the records of prior presidents. Each chapter is prefaced by one or two of President Trump's tweets related in some way to the topic of the chapter. The chapters are introduced in this way in an effort to capture the importance that Trump places on direct communication via Twitter and to demonstrate his unprecedented use of the medium. In chapter 2 we explore Donald Trump and the institutional presidency. Trump's use of appointments, organization of the White House, and use of the unilateral instruments of presidential power—executive orders, signing statements, and presidential memoranda—receive thorough description at the outset of the chapter. A central focus is the impact of Trump's personality on these presidential behaviors. The chapter concludes with a discussion of the degree to which Trump used the opportunities available to him at the outset of his presidency and whether Trump has fallen victim to the "presidential power trap." We then consider whether Trump's election heralded the arrival of an opportunity to reconstruct American politics, or whether the system simply is too entrenched for any one president to deliver change (Skowronek 2011).

In chapter 3, we address the fate of Trump's ambitious legislative agenda and confirmations of his political and judicial appointees. Trump's relations with congressional parties and the role of Vice President Pence in those relationships will get particular emphasis. The later theoretical section of the chapter discusses the effect of congressional polarization upon his presidency and the differing behavioral tendencies of the House and Senate and how they affected Trump's legislative success. Much like Obama in 2009, Trump will preside over a unified federal government. Democrats rallied around President Obama, and Republicans vowed to make him a one-term president. Did Republicans rally around Trump? Did Democrats seek out common ground with Trump, or will they adopt the Republican strategy against Obama?

Donald Trump's many bold promises as a candidate are covered in chapter 4. His promises can be divided into those he can deliver under his authority as chief executive and those that will require the support of Congress. Much of President Obama's domestic policy legacy, from immigration to environmental policy, was constructed using executive orders and executive memoranda (Schier and Eberly 2013; Crews 2016). We explore President Trump's use of his power as chief executive to roll back many of those policies. Promises to build a wall along the US/Mexico border or to repeal and replace the Affordable Care Act will require support from congressional Republicans and from enough Senate Democrats to overcome likely filibuster attempts. Winning that support will require a disciplined message and a focused agenda, and early indications suggest that such discipline and focus are lacking.

In chapter 5 we review Trump's initial forays into foreign policy, especially Trump's relations with Europe, Russia, Iran, and China. Broader policies concerning international trade and environmental policies, the Middle East, and national security receive summary as well. Trump's campaign rhetoric was aggressive, and it was an open question whether that rhetoric would be matched by equally assertive policies. The chapter concludes with consideration of whether Trump is acting as a "realist" or a "liberal" in his foreign policy stewardship.

In the final chapter we consider the evidence gathered in previous chapters to discuss Trump's future prospects regarding his relations with his party, the media, public support, congressional relations, presidential governance, domestic policy, and foreign policy. Beyond this, which Trump actions seem most consequential to the remainder of his presidency? Trump entered the presidency with no prior experience in public office and may face a steep learning curve during his first year. Are there clear lessons that he has learned? Can a Donald Trump presidency comport well with America's traditional democratic practices?

WORKS CITED

Ahmadian, Sara, Sara Azarshahi, and Delroy L. Paulhus. "Explaining Donald Trump via Communication Style: Grandiosity, Informality, and Dynamism." *Personality and Individual Differences* 107 (March 2017): 49–53. doi:10.1016/j.paid.2016.11.018.

Blanton, Dana. "Fox News Poll: Voters Say Trump's Tweets Hurting Agenda." Fox News. June 29, 2017. Accessed July 9, 2017. http://www.foxnews.com/politics/2017/06/29/fox-news-poll-voters-say-trumps-tweets-hurting-agenda.html.

Chozick, Amy. "Hillary Clinton Blames F.B.I. Director for Election Loss." *New York Times*. November 12, 2016. Accessed March 17, 2017. https://www.nytimes.com/2016/11/13/us/politics/hillary-clinton-james-comey.html?smprod=nytcore-iphone&smid=nytcore-iphone-share.

Cohn, Nate. "A 2016 Review: There's Reason to Be Skeptical of a Comey Effect." *New York Times*. May 8, 2017. Accessed July 9, 2017. https://www.nytimes.com/2017/05/08/upshot/a-2016-review-theres-reason-to-be-skeptical-of-a-comey-effect.html.

Crews, Clydes. "Obama's Legacy: An Abundance of Executive Actions." *Forbes.* January 10, 2016. Accessed July 8, 2017. https://www.forbes.com/sites/ waynecrews/2016/01/10/this-inventory-of-obamas-dozens-of-executive-actions -frames-his-final-state-of-the-union-address/#401106a875f5.

Desk, NBC News Exit Poll. "NBC News Exit Poll: Trump Dominates among Working-Class Whites." NBCNews.com. November 9, 2016. Accessed July 8, 2017. http://www.nbcnews.com/storyline/data-points/nbc-news-exit-poll -trump-dominates-among-working-class-whites-n681146.

Devine, Christopher J., and Kyle C. Kopko. "5 Things You Need to Know about How Third-Party Candidates Did in 2016." *Washington Post.* November 15, 2016. Accessed July 10, 2017. https://www.washingtonpost.com/news/monkey -cage/wp/2016/11/15/5-things-you-need-to-know-about-how-third-party-candi dates-did-in-2016/?utm_term=.80f072ed9b24.

Enten, Harry. "Why Clinton's Electoral Map Isn't as Good as Obama's." FiveThirtyEight. September 16, 2016. Accessed July 6, 2017. http://fivethirty eight.com/features/why-clintons-electoral-map-isnt-as-good-as-obamas/.

Ferrechio, Susan. "Democrats Kick off Anti-Trump 'Resistance Summer.'" *Washington Examiner.* June 1, 2017. Accessed July 9, 2017. http://www.wash ingtonexaminer.com/democrats-kick-off-anti-trump-resistance-summer/article /2624624.

Gallup, Inc. "Gallup Daily: Trump Job Approval." Gallup.com. Accessed July 9, 2017. http://www.gallup.com/poll/201617/gallup-daily-trump-job-approval .aspx.

Grim, Ryan. "Nate Silver Is Unskewing Polls—All of Them. Here's How." Huff-ington Post. November 7, 2016. Accessed July 6, 2017. http://www.huffington post.com/entry/nate-silver-election-forecast_us_581e1c33e4b0d9ce6fbc6f7f.

Inzaurralde, Bastien. "Analysis | This Linguist Studied the Way Trump Speaks for Two Years. Here's What She Found." *Washington Post.* July 7, 2017. Accessed July 8, 2017. https://www.washingtonpost.com/news/the-fix/wp/2017/07/07/this -linguist-studied-the-way-trump-speaks-for-two-years-heres-what-she-found/? utm_term=.2ecd77ba22d4.

Jackson, Natalie, and Adam Hooper. "2016 President Forecast." Huffington Post. October 3, 2016. Accessed March 17, 2017. http://elections.huffingtonpost.com/ 2016/forecast/president.

Judis, John. "The Emerging Republican Advantage." *National Journal.* January 30, 2015. Accessed July 8, 2017. https://www.nationaljournal.com/s/32748/ emerging-republican-advantage.

Judis, John B., and Ruy Teixeira. "The Emerging Democratic Majority." *New York Times.* November 24, 2002. Accessed July 8, 2017. http://www.nytimes .com/2002/11/24/books/chapters/the-emerging-democratic-majority.html.

Katz, Josh. "2016 Election Forecast: Who Will Be President?" *New York Times*. July 19, 2016. Accessed March 17, 2017. https://www.nytimes.com/interactive /2016/upshot/presidential-polls-forecast.html?_r=0.

Klinkner, Philip A., and Thomas Schaller. "LBJ's Revenge: The 2008 Election and the Rise of the Great Society Coalition." *The Forum* 6, no. 4 (January 2009). doi:10.2202/1540-8884.1269.

Kopan, Tal. "What Donald Trump Has Said about Mexico." CNN. August 31, 2016. Accessed July 10, 2017. http://edition.cnn.com/2016/08/31/politics/ donald-trump-mexico-statements/index.html.

Kristof, Nicholas. "Opinion | My Shared Shame: The Media Helped Make Trump." *New York Times*. March 26, 2016. Accessed July 6, 2017. https://www .nytimes.com/2016/03/27/opinion/sunday/my-shared-shame-the-media-helped -make-trump.html?_r=0.

Kurtzleben, Danielle. "Pollsters Find 'At Best Mixed Evidence' Comey Letter Swayed Election." NPR. May 5, 2017. Accessed July 9, 2017. http://www.npr .org/2017/05/05/526936636/pollsters-find-at-best-mixed-evidence-comey -letter-swayed-election.

Luhby, Tami. "Obamacare Premiums to Soar 22% on Average." CNNMoney. October 24, 2016. Accessed July 9, 2017. http://money.cnn.com/2016/10/24/ news/economy/obamacare-premiums/.

Mann, Thomas E. "What Do the Models Say about Who Will Win in November?" Brookings Institution. September 15, 2016. Accessed July 6, 2017. https://www .brookings.edu/blog/fixgov/2016/09/15/what-do-the-models-say-about-who -will-win-in-november/.

McLaughlin, Dan. "The Real Reason Trump Won: Part 1 of 4." *National Review*. January 10, 2017a. Accessed July 10, 2017. http://www.nationalreview.com/ article/443687/barack-obama-real-reason-trump-won.

McLaughlin, Dan. "The Real Reason Trump Won: Part 4 of 4." *National Review*. January 17, 2017b. Accessed July 10, 2017. http://www.nationalreview.com/ article/443909/real-reason-trump-won-trend-away-incumbents-strongest-factor.

Mead, Walter Russell. "RIP, 'Emerging Democratic Majority.'" The American Interest. February 2, 2015. Accessed July 9, 2017. https://www.the-american -interest.com/2015/02/02/rip-emerging-democratic-majority/.

NateSilver538. "2016 Election Forecast." FiveThirtyEight. November 8, 2016a. Accessed March 17, 2017. https://projects.fivethirtyeight.com/2016-election -forecast/.

NateSilver538. "Election Update: Why Clinton's Position Is Worse Than Obama's." FiveThirtyEight. November 4, 2016b. Accessed July 6, 2017. https://fivethirtyeight .com/features/election-update-why-clintons-position-is-worse-than-obamas/.

NateSilver538. "Election Update: Yes, Donald Trump Has a Path to Victory." FiveThirtyEight. November 2, 2016c. Accessed March 17, 2017. http://fivethirty eight.com/features/election-update-yes-donald-trump-has-a-path-to-victory/.

Page, Susan, and Brad Heath. "How Anti-establishment Outsider Donald Trump Was Elected the 45th President of the United States." *USA Today*. November 9, 2016. Accessed July 6, 2017. https://www.usatoday.com/story/news/politics/elections/2016/11/09/election-analysis-hillary-clinton-donald-trump/93198882/.

Patterson, Thomas E. "News Coverage of the 2016 General Election: How the Press Failed the Voters." Shorenstein Center. December 7, 2016a. Accessed July 6, 2017. http://shorensteincenter.org/news-coverage-2016-general-election/.

Patterson, Thomas E. "News Coverage of the 2016 National Conventions: Negative News, Lacking Context." Shorenstein Center. December 7, 2016b. Accessed July 6, 2017. http://shorensteincenter.org/news-coverage-2016-national-conventions/.

Patterson, Thomas E. "News Coverage of the 2016 Presidential Primaries: Horse Race Reporting Has Consequences." Shorenstein Center. December 7, 2016c. Accessed July 6, 2017. https://shorensteincenter.org/news-coverage-2016-presidential-primaries/.

Patterson, Thomas E. "Pre-Primary News Coverage of the 2016 Presidential Race: Trump's Rise, Sanders' Emergence, Clinton's Struggle." Shorenstein Center. December 7, 2016d. Accessed July 6, 2017. https://shorensteincenter.org/pre-primary-news-coverage-2016-trump-clinton-sanders/.

"Presidential National Exit Poll 2016." *Exit Polls 2016*, CNN. November 9, 2016.

Ranzini, Stephen. "The 'Overton Window' and How Trump Won the Nomination with It." *The Hill*. October 1, 2016. Accessed July 8, 2017. http://thehill.com/blogs/pundits-blog/presidential-campaign/298417-the-overton-window-and-how-trump-won-the-nomination.

Rucker, Philip. "'I Would Be Your President': Clinton Blames Russia, FBI Chief for 2016 Election Loss." *Washington Post*. May 3, 2017. Accessed July 9, 2017. https://www.washingtonpost.com/politics/hillary-clinton-blames-russian-hackers-and-comey-for-2016-election-loss/2017/05/02/e62fef72-2f60-11e7-8674-437ddb6e813e_story.html?utm_term=.66b77b95b9d4.

Rucker, Philip. "Trump Says Fox's Megyn Kelly Had 'Blood Coming Out of Her Wherever.'" *Washington Post*. August 8, 2015. Accessed July 10, 2017. https://www.washingtonpost.com/news/post-politics/wp/2015/08/07/trump-says-foxs-megyn-kelly-had-blood-coming-out-of-her-wherever/?utm_term=.8048c1c2f1d2.

Sasson, Eric. "Blame Trump's Victory on College-Educated Whites, Not the Working Class." *New Republic*. November 15, 2016. Accessed July 8, 2017. https://newrepublic.com/article/138754/blame-trumps-victory-college-educated-whites-not-working-class.

Schier, Steven E., and Todd E. Eberly. *American Government and Popular Discontent: Stability without Success*. New York: Routledge, 2013.

Sclafani, Jennifer. *Talking Donald Trump: A Sociolinguistic Study of Style, Metadiscourse, and Political Identity*. S.l.: Routledge, 2017.

Sheth, Sonam, and Natasha Bertrand. "Evidence Is Mounting That Russia Took 4 Clear Paths to Meddle in the US Election." *Business Insider*. June 24, 2017. Accessed July 9, 2017. http://www.businessinsider.com/evidence-russia-meddled -in-us-election-2017-6.

Skowronek, Stephen. *Presidential Leadership in Political Time: Reprisal and Reappraisal*. 2nd ed. Lawrence: University Press of Kansas, 2011.

Teixeira, Ruy. "The Emerging Democratic Majority Turns 10." *The Atlantic*. November 9, 2012. Accessed July 8, 2017. https://www.theatlantic.com/politics/ archive/2012/11/the-emerging-democratic-majority-turns-10/265005/.

Trende, Sean, and David Byler. "How Trump Won—Conclusions." RealClear-Politics. January 20, 2017. Accessed July 9, 2017. https://www.realclearpolitics .com/articles/2017/01/20/how_trump_won_--_conclusions_132846.html.

"Trump Wiretapping Claim: Did Obama Bug His Successor?" BBC News. March 20, 2017. Accessed July 10, 2017. http://www.bbc.com/news/world-us -canada-39172635.

Waldman, Paul. "Opinion | Can Donald Trump Do an Extreme General Election Makeover?" *Washington Post*. March 10, 2016. Accessed July 9, 2017. https:// www.washingtonpost.com/blogs/plum-line/wp/2016/03/10/can-donald-trump -do-an-extreme-general-election-makeover/.

Watkins, Eli. "Bill Clinton Meeting Causes Headaches for Hillary." CNN. June 30, 2016. Accessed July 9, 2017. http://edition.cnn.com/2016/06/29/politics/ bill-clinton-loretta-lynch/index.html.

Wootson, Cleve R., Jr. "Analysis | Trump Says His Tweets Are 'Modern Day Presidential.' We Checked with Other Modern-Day Leaders." *Washington Post*. July 2, 2017. Accessed July 9, 2017. https://www.washingtonpost.com/news/world views/wp/2017/07/02/trump-says-his-tweets-are-modern-day-presidential-we -checked-with-other-modern-day-presidents/?utm_term=.5a0d1b383e67.

2

Trump in the President's Office

@realDonaldTrump
Don't let the FAKE NEWS tell you that there is big infighting in the
Trump Admin. We are getting along great, and getting major things done!
(9:14 a.m., March 7, 2017)

The institution of the presidency has several aspects. It reaches beyond
the president's Oval Office to the Executive Office of the President
(EOP), a series of presidential bureaucracies employing about four thousand people. Most prominent within the EOP are three organizations.

Closest to the president is the White House Office that includes top
staff in charge of media relations, congressional relations, policy planning, and executive branch appointments. The president's Office of Management and Budget (OMB), employing 529 people, performs a variety
of "prime ministerial" functions for the president. These include compos-
ing his annual budget proposal, improving management in the executive
branch, recommending vetoes, and "legislative clearance"—determining
which policy ideas from the executive branch go to Congress as presidential proposals.

Two other major EOP organizations are the National Security Council
that meets regularly to assess and manage security threats to the nation.
Its statutory members include the president, vice president, and the secretaries of the Departments of State, Defense, and Energy, along with

other officials invited by the president. The head of the council's staff, the national security advisor, is a top presidential aide who also attends all meeting of the council.

Beyond the EOP lie the fifteen departments of the president's cabinet. The Department of Health and Human Services, with its administration of the massive Social Security (retirement income), Medicare (retiree health care), and Medicaid (health care for the poor), has the largest budget. The Department of Defense has the largest number of employees. The Departments of Justice and Treasury deal with law enforcement and financial management, respectively, and are two of the oldest departments. The other departments have authority over particular areas of domestic policy: Veterans Affairs, Transportation, Housing and Urban Development, Commerce, Education, Energy, Homeland Security, Agriculture, and Interior. All told, the cabinet departments employ about 4,214,000 employees. Most do not work in Washington, DC, but in regional field offices spread throughout the United States.

This is a big management challenge, far greater and more complex than Donald Trump's personal business enterprises. Trump also has to contend with an imposing list of presidential leadership roles that all modern presidents since Franklin Roosevelt (1932–1945) have undertaken. Clinton Rossiter enumerated these back in 1956: leader of the executive branch, Congress, public opinion, armed forces, international leader of free nations, and ceremonial head of state (Rossiter 1956).

That is a lot to unpack and for any one president to undertake. In understanding a presidency, though, it is best to start with the president himself. His personality and individual behaviors cast great influence on the American government and international relations. What do we know about Donald Trump's personal traits that will help us understand his presidency?

DONALD TRUMP THE PERSON

An individual's personality is an OCEAN. That's an acronym for the "five-factor personality model" that is widely used in psychology. In this theory, people are characterized by their personal manifestations of the traits of (O) openness to experience, (C) conscientiousness, (E) extroversion, (A) agreeableness, and (N) neuroticism.

Those open to experience are original, creative, intellectual, and have wide interests in contrast to those with commonplace, simple, and conforming habits. Conscientious people are thorough, dependable, precise, and hardworking, unlike those who are lazy, careless, distractible, and irresponsible. Extroverted people are energetic, talkative, assertive, and outspoken as opposed to those who are low-key, reserved, and shy. Agreeable people are trusting, moderate, and considerate, unlike those who are stubborn, ruthless, demanding, and uncooperative. Neurotic people are moody, tense, self-conscious, and have trouble controlling their impulses in contrast to calm, relaxed, and secure individuals (Rubenzer and Faschingbauer 2004, 7–16).

How does Trump rank regarding these traits? Psychologist Dan P. McAdams assessed Trump's personality in the midst of the candidate's 2016 presidential campaign. By 2016, Trump had been in the public eye for more than thirty years, forging a well-known personality. McAdams described Trump thusly: "Across his lifetime, Donald Trump has exhibited a trait profile that you would not expect of a U.S. president: sky-high extroversion combined with off-the-chart low agreeableness" (McAdams 2016). What motivates this volatile combination? According to McAdams, anger: "Anger can fuel malice, but it can also motivate social dominance, stoking a desire to win the adoration of others. Combined with a considerable gift for humor (which may also be aggressive), anger lies at the heart of Trump's charisma. And anger permeates his political rhetoric" (McAdams 2016). Trump, per McAdams, also has low openness to experiences.

This does not, however, predict disaster due to Trump's personality. McAdams notes that Trump's long experience as a "deal maker" may make him a flexible and pragmatic decision maker, and his ideological flexibility may prove to be an asset in negotiating with Congress and foreign governments. But the looming problem is Trump's low agreeableness, which has already put him in the midst of several fights early in his presidency—with the media, with Democrats, and with James Comey, the fired FBI director.

Trump's traits closely resemble those of "dominator" presidents, so classified by Steven Rubenzer and Thomas Faschingbauer in their landmark study of presidential personality (Rubenzer and Faschingbauer 2004). The dominators of presidential history were Andrew Jackson, Lyndon Johnson, and Richard Nixon: "They were exceptionally bossy, demanding, domineering, manipulative; none was even tempered. All acted assertively, were self-centered and egotistical, stubborn and hardheaded and thought highly of themselves" (Rubenzer and Faschingbauer 2004, 83). Trump seems to share many of these traits. He has even installed a portrait of Andrew Jackson, whom he admires, in the White House.

How might a dominator like Trump govern? His dominator predecessors all ranked low on personal character, high in neuroticism, and very low on openness and agreeableness. Since Trump shares these traits, his presidency is likely to continue to be a jarring ride.

Trump's aggressiveness and frequent tweets have produced many controversies over the truthfulness of his assertions. The media challenges many of his statements as factually untruthful. The *Washington Post*'s fact checking has identified numerous instances of "false and misleading claims" during his first six months in office. Many of his tweets—limited to 140 characters—understandably "lack context." An example is a June 5 tweet in which he refers to his immigration executive order as a "TRAVEL BAN" despite the fact that his administration previously had stated that the order was not a travel ban (*Washington Post* 2017a). On April 29 he tweeted, "We have an all-time record for the biggest increase in the stock market." In fact, the early months of George W. Bush's presidency witnessed a larger increase than occurred in 2017 (*Washington Post* 2017a).

Trump's embellishments of the factual record have long been part of his approach in business. In his 1987 book *The Art of the Deal* he described it this way: "The final key to the way I promote is bravado. I play to people's fantasies. People may not always think big themselves, but they can still get very excited by those who do. That's why a little hyperbole never hurts. People want to believe that something is the biggest and the greatest and the most spectacular. I call it truthful hyperbole. It's an innocent form of exaggeration—and a very effective form of promotion" (Trump 1987, 58). Given the nation's polarized politics, not everyone views Trump's exaggerations as innocent. The low agreeableness and character of the dominator are evident in such behavior, portending a bumpy path for Donald Trump in the White House.

THE TRUMP TRANSITION TO THE PRESIDENCY

There were indeed some bumps along the way for Trump from Election Day on November 8 to his inauguration on January 20, 2017. Trump's loss of the popular vote by a 2.1 percentage point margin while winning the Electoral College ignited considerable public controversy. Democratic "blue America" responded with outrage, public demonstrations, demands for recounts, legal challenges to Trump electors, and pleas to Trump state electors to disregard their state's popular vote when electing the next president.

Despite the turbulence, the transition period offered Trump important opportunities. Martha Joynt Kumar, a transition scholar, notes that "an effective transition buys a new administration the chance to take advantage of the opportunities that exist at the beginning of an administration and to reduce the number of inevitable hazards. The benefits range from the direction of government to the reputation a president establishes in the early days" (Keegan 2015).

Actual transition planning had begun months earlier than Election Day. The Trump and Clinton campaigns were beneficiaries of the Presidential Transitions Act of 2010, which for the first time allowed the campaigns to run transition operations with government support months before Election Day. On May 6, once he had locked up the 2016 Republican nomination, Trump asked his son-in-law, Jared Kushner, to start planning the transition. Three days later, the candidate announced that New Jersey Governor Chris Christie, a 2016 rival for the GOP nomination who later endorsed Trump, would head the transition effort. By October, the transition staff numbered more than 100 and included many policy experts added to compensate for a dearth of them on the campaign staff (Restuccia and Cook 2016).

On November 11, Trump instigated a big shakeup of the transition staff. He ousted Chris Christie and many of his transition subordinates, apparently dissatisfied with the pace of the transition and Christie's involvement in the "Bridgegate" corruption scandal in his home state. The change was abrupt, with the Christie-appointed staffers quickly shown the exit and in one case at least, locked out of the transition office (Dilanian and Jaffe 2016). Vice President–elect Pence took over supervision of the transition. A steady announcement of major administration appointments resulted in the ensuing weeks.

Trump's top appointees proved to be diverse in background but less demographically diverse than those of his predecessor, Barack Obama. Trump's cabinet included only three women—Betsy DeVos at Education, Elaine Chao at Transportation (secretary of labor under George W. Bush and spouse of Senate Majority Leader Mitch McConnell), and UN ambassador Nikki Haley. Trump's rival for the 2016 GOP nomination, physician Ben Carson, became the only African American in the cabinet as secretary of housing and urban development. Alexander Acosta, dean of Florida International University law school, became the first Latino member of Trump's cabinet as secretary of labor.

Retired generals populated Trump's national security team. Defense Secretary James Mattis, a retired four-star army general and former commander of the US Central Command, directed US forces in the Middle East from 2010 to 2013. A retired four-star Marine Corps general, Homeland Security Secretary John Kelly had headed the US Southern Command from 2012 to 2016. Kelly eventually succeeded Reince Priebus as White House chief of staff. National Security Advisor H. R. McMaster, a retired three-star army general, pioneered innovative battlefield tactics during the Iraq war. Trump's reliance on the generals reflected his stout praise of the US military during the 2016 campaign, an allegiance probably born of his happy years as a teenage student at New York Military Academy. Unlike cabinet appointments, the national security advisor does not require Senate confirmation.

Before McMaster, a particularly controversial appointment was three-star general Mike Flynn as the president's national security advisor, who heads a presidential staff of national security analysts. Flynn had endorsed and campaigned for Trump after being fired as head of the Defense Intelligence Agency under Obama. Flynn was dismissed by Trump in mid-February after Vice President Pence asserted that Flynn had failed to disclose important information about Flynn's meeting with the Russian ambassador in Washington.

A successful appointment as director of national intelligence went to former GOP senator Dan Coats of Indiana. The director sits on the president's cabinet and National Security Council. Representative Mike Pompeo of California received appointment to the important non-cabinet post of CIA director. Both Coats and Pompeo served on their chamber's Select Committee on Intelligence and have established "hawkish" positions on national security issues.

Trump's diplomatic appointments brought far less relevant experience to their new jobs than did the generals. Secretary of State Rex Tillerson, like Trump, had no prior governmental experience. He began a lengthy career in international business as an engineer and rose to become chief executive officer of the Exxon international corporation. UN ambassador Nikki Haley was in her second term as South Carolina governor when appointed to her position, which carries cabinet rank. It was initially unclear how these appointees would shape the nation's overseas diplomacy.

In contrast to Trump's populist pronouncements on the campaign stump, his economic policy appointees hailed from Wall Street and the conservative Washington establishment. Treasury Secretary Steve Mnuchin worked for Goldman Sachs for seventeen years and later for other New York investment firms. Commerce Secretary Wilbur Ross was founder and president of the W. L. Ross and Company investment firm. Investment banker Gary Cohn became the president's chief economic advisor and chair of his National Economic Council. The chair of the president's Council of Economic Advisors, Kevin Hasset, came from the American Enterprise Institute, a beltway think tank populated by many establishment conservatives. Another conventional Washington nominee was David Shulkin as secretary of veterans affairs. Shulkin had served as undersecretary of health in that department in the Obama administration.

Three members of Congress also entered the Trump cabinet. Montana representative Ryan Zinke became the first Montanan to serve as interior secretary. Physician and Georgia representative Tom Price took charge of the massive Department of Health and Human Services, the department with the largest annual budget. Price had authored a GOP alternative to Obama's Affordable Care Act (Obamacare) and became a central player in Trump's efforts to restructure federal health-care programs. Senator Jeff Sessions of Alabama, the first senator to endorse Trump's 2016 candidacy, took the reins of the Department of Justice as attorney general. Sessions's approach to justice issues marked a stark departure from Obama administration positions.

Three other cabinet appointees had considerable governmental experience, if not Washington experience. Energy Secretary Rick Perry had served two terms as GOP governor of Texas. As a 2016 presidential candidate, he had called for the abolition of the department but recanted that position upon being nominated to the post. Sonny Perdue, former Republican governor of Georgia, became secretary of agriculture. Oklahoma attorney general Scott Pruitt was named head of the Environmental Protection Agency, a regulatory body he had frequently criticized and litigated against in court on behalf of his state.

Most nominees were not welcomed by Democratic senators. Minority Leader Charles Schumer (NY) sought to slow down the confirmation process as his partisan colleagues scrutinized nominees thoroughly during confirmation hearings. Democrats temporarily boycotted confirmation hearings for Price and Mnuchin, arguing that their financial backgrounds needed further investigation. Two other appointees encountered particularly turbulent Senate confirmations and very close—though successful—confirmation votes: Sessions and DeVos.

The Sessions nomination became entangled in allegations of racial bias during his service as attorney general of Alabama. The controversial

Trump executive order on immigration, subject to enforcement by the Justice Department, also drew much controversy to the Sessions nomination. Sessions nevertheless gained approval in party line votes in the Senate Judiciary Committee and the Senate floor.

Democrats challenged DeVos about her lack of background on education issues and her past advocacy of school choice or "vouchers" for private schools. She would be the first secretary of education who had never attended, taught in, or sent her children to public schools and so faced tough questions at Senate hearings. A party line vote in the Senate Health, Education, Labor, and Pensions Committee sent her nomination to the floor. Vice President Pence as president of the Senate had to break a 50–50 vote on the Senate floor to get DeVos confirmed. Moderate Republican senators Lisa Murkowski (AK) and Susan Collins (ME) voted against DeVos, citing concerns over her support for public education.

What do these top nominees reveal about Trump as president? His esteem for the generals led him to delegate decision-making authority over military strikes to his commanders shortly after he took office. A Pentagon spokesman stated in early March, "This was an authority that was delegated by the president, through the secretary of defense to the Central Command commander to carry out" (Greenwood 2017). Obama, in contrast, maintained thorough operational control over military strikes.

The same tendency to delegate was not evident initially with his diplomatic appointments. Secretary of State Tillerson kept an unusually low profile in the early months of the administration. The initial Trump budget proposed severe cuts in the State Department budget while significantly boosting military spending. The president often took the initiative in stating major themes of his foreign policy in speeches both domestic and overseas and, of course, in his evening tweets. At times he contradicted the policy statements of UN ambassador Haley.

Trump's economic policies, aside from trade, very much reflected conventional Republican thinking. In late April, Steve Mnuchin and Gary Cohn released a one-page outline of the administration's tax plan. Its reductions in marginal personal income tax rates, estate taxes, and the corporate income tax reflected long-established GOP goals. On trade, Trump withdrew from the Trans-Pacific Partnership negotiated by Obama. He continued to criticize Germany and China for their huge balance of trade surpluses with the United States while also pledging to renegotiate the North America Free Trade Agreement (NAFTA) to get better terms from Canada and Mexico.

Trump's "justice agenda" coincided with Jeff Sessions's priorities, auguring new restrictions on immigration, more aggressive immigration enforcement, and a steady stream of conservative judicial nominees. Tom Price at HHS quickly became a major player in the high-profile attempt to repeal or revise Obama's Affordable Care Act. The other domestic cabinet secretaries proved to be lower-profile figures during the administration's first months, reflecting their departmental agendas' reduced standing among the administration's priorities.

The administration proved very slow in making lower-level executive branch appointments. These include the four top levels of each cabinet department (secretary, deputy assistant secretaries, and undersecretaries), ambassadors to foreign nations, and heads of independent agencies and members of regulatory commissions. As of late July 2017, Trump had nominated only 146 individuals for the 570 key appointed positions requiring Senate confirmation. Of these, a meager 46 had been confirmed and taken office. By late May in his first term, Obama in contrast had nominated 368 persons with 203 already confirmed. The average time between nomination and confirmation for Trump appointees was 45 days, compared to 37 for Obama appointees (*Washington Post* 2017b).

The president blamed the slow pace of confirmations on Senate Democrats, who "used procedural measures to force the full length of time allowed for nearly all nominees, slowing down the process considerably" (Kopan 2017). The lengthy appointment process for top officials helped to slow the selection of appointees for positions below them in their organizations. That does not, however, explain fully the slow pace of nominations. Trump the outsider lacked an established network of Washington allies who could suggest nominees and facilitate their administration approval. Trump's transition had also been slow off the mark, further delaying nominations. Laggard nominations blunted the impact of the "Trump revolution" in Washington by missing the available momentum during his early months in the White House.

TRUMP AND HIS WHITE HOUSE STAFF

A major locus of media-centered drama during Trump's early presidency has been the turbulence surrounding the operations of his White House staff. Unlike Obama, George W. Bush, and most recent presidents, Trump eschewed a "gatekeeper" who would limit access to the president and thus add shape and contour to the administration's agenda. Though Reince Priebus, 2016 national GOP party chair, became White House chief of staff, it quickly became clear that Trump would operate independently in communicating with the public—often by smartphone tweets—and pursuing his personal presidential agenda. Trump in effect became a media freelancer within his own administration.

Trump daily granted presidential access to a wide variety of staff people. His Oval Office is often populated by many underlings, in marked contrast to the more introverted Obama, who kept the office quiet and access to it tightly regulated by his chief of staff. *Time* magazine sketched this portrait of the Trump Oval Office in April 2017:

> In a few minutes, President Donald Trump will release a new set of tweets, flooding social-media accounts with his unique brand of digital smelling salts—words that will jolt his supporters and provoke his adversaries. Nearly a dozen senior aides stand in the Oval Office, crowding behind couches or near door-length windows. This is the way he likes to work, more often than not: in a crowd. He sits behind his desk finishing the tasks of the day, which have included watching new Senate testimony about Russian involvement in the 2016 presidential election, by signing orders in red folders with a black Sharpie. (Scherer and Miller 2017)

Trump's at times volatile temperament, in combination with the loose organizational structure of his White House, led to an atmosphere of fear, spawning many leaks from his staff. This led to a steady stream of media stories as Priebus, senior counselor Steve Bannon, counselor Kellyanne Conway, daughter Ivanka and her husband, senior advisor Jared Kushner, were portrayed as constantly jockeying for position. The "who's up, who's down" media stories provided an at times annoying distraction for the administration. The appointment of John Kelly as chief of staff, replacing Priebus at the end of July, potentially augured a more orderly flow of information and staff to the president.

Trump's first press secretary, Sean Spicer, formerly the press spokesperson for the Republican National Committee, was a particular target of rumors. Trump, ever concerned about personal appearance, early on directed him to get new suits and at times was reported to be quite critical of Spicer's press conference performances. But Spicer had the toughest job in Washington. At times the press office would provide a rationale for an administration action only to have that rationale contradicted by a presidential tweet.

The challenges facing the White House press office crested during a Trump-generated administration crisis, the firing of FBI Director James Comey. Spicer and his assistant press secretary, Sarah Huckabee Sanders, initially stated that the president had "no choice" but to fire Comey based on a memo written by Deputy Attorney General Rod Rosenstein. According to Spicer, the firing was really Rosenstein's doing—"all him" (Saletan 2017). Shortly afterward, Trump in an interview contradicted them, claiming that he had long intended to fire Comey "regardless" of what the Justice Department recommended, terming Comey a "showboat" and "grandstander" (Pramuk 2017). The White House had shifted from "no drama Obama" to "constant drama Trump." In July, Spicer resigned upon learning that Anthony Scaramucci, a Wall Street investor with no experience in media relations, would become his boss as White House director of communications. Scaramucci's 250-hour tenure in the position ended when his profanity-laden interview with journalist Ryan Lizza led to his dismissal by the new chief of staff, John Kelly. The position of communications director remained vacant for weeks after the dismissal.

Trump kept the White House atmosphere charged through his treatment of his staff associates. "Trump prefers a management style in which even compliments can come laced with a bite, and where enduring snubs and belittling jokes, even in public, is part of the job," according to the *Washington Post* (Parker 2017). This "dominator" behavior is remarkably similar to that of Lyndon Johnson, who frequently scorned his staff, at times meeting with an aide while sitting on the toilet (Frady 2002). Having one's staff scampering like scared rabbits has its costs for a president. Fear of one's boss can prevent important but unwelcome information from coming his way and promotes unhelpful leaks. Both problems seem likely to persist in Trump's White House.

NORMAL AND ABNORMAL IN THE EARLY TRUMP ADMINISTRATION

In the midst of White House turbulence, a pattern of "creeping normality" in presidential operations did begin to appear after the administration's abnormally tumultuous initial weeks. Trump's term began with a controversial ban on immigration from seven Middle Eastern countries that quickly was overruled by federal courts and withdrawn. This was an executive order, an official presidential directive about how executive branch officials are to conduct their duties. The orders have the status of law unless rescinded by a later president or voided by federal courts. The ban had not been vetted by the Department of Homeland Security or Department of Defense but had been the quick work of White House aides Bannon and Stephen Miller. It was eventually withdrawn and a revised order promulgated, again voided by the courts and headed to the Supreme Court for final resolution later in 2017. The Supreme Court preliminarily reinstated the travel ban in June 2017 but required broader exemptions from the ban for relatives of individuals living in the United States (Barnes 2017).

The *New York Times* assembled a panel of thirteen experts from academe and government to assess the "normality" of the Trump administration's actions during its first two months in office. They rated a majority of the first month's actions, fifteen of nineteen actions, as abnormal and twelve of these as abnormal and particularly important. The abnormal and highly important actions included the immigration executive orders and an executive order for a border wall with Mexico, secret conflict of interest waivers for White House aides, appointing daughter Ivanka as a White House advisor, and the slow pace of administration appointments. Most of the abnormal and important actions, however, involved statements by the White House and by Trump himself. They included harsh criticism of the press by the president and his aides, including enunciation of the concepts of "alternative facts" and "fake news." Remarkable presidential tweets made the list as well: Trump claimed that "millions" of fraudulent votes were cast of Election Day 2016, asserted that Obama had ordered wiretaps of Trump's phone, criticized federal judges for their immigration decisions, and tweeted frequently and provocatively about foreign affairs.

In Trump's second month, White House operations began to better resemble the normal operations of previous presidencies. A series of important policies were announced and pursued in a conventional way. These included the administration's budget proposal, tax plan, and introduction of the American Health Care Act repealing Obamacare. Also more ordinary were Trump's announcement that NATO was no longer "obsolete," his reversal of his previous intent to label China a "currency manipulator," and a cruise missile strike on Syria. Amid these more conventional behaviors, however, Trump continued his often rash and intemperate tweets and invited a major controversy by firing FBI director Comey (Bui, Miller, and Qualey 2017).

ETHICS QUESTIONS SURROUNDING TRUMP

Another unusual aspect of the early Trump presidency was its handling of ethics questions. During the 2016 campaign, candidate Trump made several promises to clean up the Washington "swamp." His "Contract with the American Voter" included promises to place a five-year ban on White House and congressional officials becoming lobbyists, a lifetime ban on White House officials lobbying for foreign governments, and a complete ban on foreign lobbyists raising money for US elections. Several such reforms would be included in the "Clean Up Corruption in Washington" act that he would submit to Congress ("Donald Trump's Contract" 2016).

Candidate Trump nevertheless received criticism regarding several ethics issues arising from his distinctive financial position and holdings. Presidential scholar Barbara Perry noted in 2015 that he "stands out because he is not just a businessman. He's the Flo Ziegfeld or P.T. Barnum of politics. He's an impresario. He's genuinely unique" (Schouten 2015). His uniqueness was defined by his net worth, which he claimed was $10 billion during the campaign but was estimated at $3.5 billion in 2017 by *Forbes* magazine (*Forbes* 2017).

How does a person with such extensive financial holdings prevent his investments from influencing his presidential decisions? Walter Schaub, director of the Office of Governmental Ethics, argued that nothing short of total divestiture would erase the ethical concerns created by Trump's wealth. Divestiture "would mean the sale of all of the president's assets, with their value conveyed to a blind trust—and an investment portfolio of which he and his family would have no knowledge or control" (Hopkins 2017).

Trump would have none of that. In January, he announced arrangements that he claimed addressed the ethical concerns surrounding his wealth. Trump agreed to give up his position as an officer of the Trump organization, pledging no communication with it beyond regular receipt of profit and loss statements. His sons, Donald Jr. and Eric, along with company executive Alan Weisselberg would take over management of the organization. The president-elect also canceled all pending international deals with his organization. His lawyer, Sherri Dillon, argued, "President Trump can't unknow he owns Trump Tower," and he "should not be expected to destroy the company he built" (Harwell 2017).

Schaub and other ethics experts termed Trump's approach totally inadequate. Richard Painter, ethics counsel in the George W. Bush White House, worried that "the setup will not prevent Trump from knowing his business' sources of revenue or block him from receiving income from the trust" (Harwell 2017). Might foreign governments try to curry favor with Trump by staying at his hotels? In April, the nonprofit group Citizens for Ethics and Responsibility in Washington filed suit in federal court arguing that Trump's arrangement violated the Constitution's "emoluments clause." Article I, Section 9, Clause 8 states, "No Title of Nobility shall be granted by the United States: And no Person holding any Office of Profit or Trust under them, shall, without the Consent of the Congress, accept of any present, Emolument, Office, or Title, of any kind whatever, from any King, Prince, or foreign State." Two lawsuits, including one by the attorneys general of Maryland and the District of Columbia, were filed claiming that because of his continuing business interests, Trump is violating the foreign emoluments clause of the Constitution (Davis 2017). Does the clause apply to the president? It remains a potentially vexing issue for the Trump administration. Should a future Democratic Congress seek to impeach Trump, this might be one of the charges used against the president.

Trump as candidate and president has not released his income tax returns, making him the first candidate to not release them since 1976. Trump's refusal also was a personal change of course. In 2012, Trump called on GOP presidential nominee Mitt Romney to release his tax returns and in 2015 indicated he would release his tax returns. Then repeatedly in early 2016, the candidate indicated that he would release his tax returns as soon as the audit they were undergoing was completed. This remains his current position (Holmes 2017).

Trump's nondisclosure is particularly striking given the breadth and complexity of his financial holdings. Disclosure would provide a field day for inquisitive journalists. It might also clarify the financial ethics of the president and perhaps quiet his critics on the issue. One such critic, Lisa Gilbert of Public Citizen, a nonprofit created by Ralph Nader, asserted, "Without complete returns, we won't know whether he owes money to foreign governments or their leaders, how much he has given in charitable contributions, how much (if anything) he has personally paid in taxes and what some of his assets really are" (Gilbert 2017).

Liberal MSNBC host Rachel Maddow drew ratings by publicizing a few pages of Trump's 2005 tax return that she had obtained, indicating he paid taxes of $35 million on an income of $150 million, a tax rate of 25.3 percent. Trump's tax rate was notably larger than the 19.6 percent rate paid by President Obama in 2015 (Roff 2017). Trump's bigger tax picture may never be revealed.

Ethics controversies also touched two Trump relatives now working in the White House: daughter Ivanka and son-in-law Jared Kushner. Kushner has a salaried job as senior advisor who has taken an oath of office and turned management of his financial affairs over to family members, though federal law bars presidents from hiring relatives to cabinet or agency jobs. A federal judge, in permitting Hillary Clinton to work in her husband's White House, ruled that it doesn't apply to White House staff jobs (Zarroli 2017).

Ivanka, however, has an office in the White House advising her father but has taken no oath of office or compensation. Like her father, who continues to own the Trump Organization while it is managed by two of his sons, Ivanka continues to own her fashion and jewelry business. Government ethics specialist Kathleen Clark, a law professor at Washington University in St. Louis, termed the Trump administration's arguments that conflict-of-interest rules don't bind the president or his daughter "disheartening. . . . My biggest concern is that this is yet another erosion of government ethics standards in this White House" (Northam and Geewax 2017).

Though President Trump promised strong ethics standards in his administration, he engendered controversy by granting "ethics waivers" to 17 White House staff members, including four former lobbyists. To "drain the swamp" of Washington, Trump prohibited senior officials hired into the executive branch from working on "particular" government matters that involve their former clients or employers for two years. Yet he waived that prohibition for some top employees. The employees included Chief of Staff Reince Priebus, counselor Kellyanne Conway, and former lobbyists working in the offices of the National Economic Council headed by Gary Cohn. In addition, a "blanket waiver" was granted to all White House staff communicating with the media, including former Breitbart media head Steve Bannon. The exemptions granted by Trump were unusually speedy and numerous. Obama granted only 17 such waivers during his eight years in office (Gold 2017).

The Trump administration's unusual ethics arrangements call into doubt his promise to "drain the swamp" in Washington. Trump, however, did attempt to follow through on two ethics promises. On January 28, 2017, he issued an executive order that required that new executive branch employees pledge that they would not lobby the particular agency they worked at within five years of the end of their employment there. The order does allow Trump to grant waivers to exempt individuals from the ban. The order further required new appointees to agree to a lifetime ban on lobbying for a foreign government. Waivers can also be issued for this ban (DeCosta-Klipa 2017). Despite these rules, however, the administration has appointed dozens of former lobbyists to "work for the agencies that they sought to influence" (Gold and Eilperin 2017).

Trump has yet send to Congress his "Clean Up Corruption in Washington" legislation, which presumably would include his promised five-year ban on White House and congressional officials becoming lobbyists after leaving office and lifetime ban on White House officials lobbying on behalf of a foreign government. He also has taken action to dilute one ethics disclosure provision in federal law. On February 14, he signed his first legislation, which repealed part of the Dodd-Frank financial regulations act that was to go into effect in 2018. It would have forced all oil, gas, and mineral companies on the US stock exchange to detail any payments they made to foreign governments. Trump's secretary of state, Rex Tillerson, the former CEO of oil and gas company Exxon-Mobil, supported repealing the legislation. Trump argued the repeal would help to create energy jobs in the United States (Yu 2017).

The repeal indicates Trump's concerns about business success and jobs can overcome previous regulations requiring public disclosure of corporate activities. It's not clear, however, how that contributes to "draining the swamp." The tensions already evident between Trump's roles as international businessperson and government reformer are certain to be evident throughout his time at 1600 Pennsylvania Avenue.

TRUMP AND RUSSIA: THE NEVER-ENDING STORY

Trump's ethics controversies received far less media attention than the ongoing revelations and investigation into the relationships of the Trump campaign and administration with the Russian government. From the evening of his surprise election victory on November 8, the topic of Trump and his campaign's relations with the Russian government and diplomats has seldom been far from the headlines. The controversy has several themes.

First, what exactly was the role of Russian hackers and the Russian government in the 2016 US election? Second, what relationships existed between Russian hackers, businesses, and the Russian government and Trump's campaign and transition staff and presidential administration? Third, what contact did Trump himself have with Russians during the campaign and since his inauguration? It's important to note that the constant stream of media stories about Trump and Russia include many from "unnamed sources" whose reliability was unclear. Some of the stories, noted later in this chronology, turned out to be false or publicly unverified.

The context for these controversies begins with public disclosure of thousands of damaging emails by the Hillary Clinton campaign during the summer and fall of the 2016 campaign. The CIA later stated that Russian officials, at the direction of President Putin, had given the emails to the WikiLeaks organization, which then publicized the stolen electronic correspondence (Reuters Staff 2017). The embarrassing disclosures certainly did not help the Clinton campaign. Other later media reports indicated that Russian military intelligence sent phishing emails to 100 local US election officials before the 2016 voting (Mindock 2017).

On July 27, 2016, days after the disclosure of thousands of Clinton campaign emails, candidate Trump called on Russia to release more of them: "Russia, if you're listening, I hope you're able to find the 30,000 emails that are missing. I think you'll be rewarded mightily by our press" (CBC 2017). On August 14, Paul Manafort, Trump's campaign chair, resigned in the wake of a *New York Times* report that he had received $12.7 million US in undisclosed payments from a pro-Russian political party in Ukraine. Manafort denied the allegations (Kramer, McIntire, and Meier 2016).

Amid growing reports of Russian election interference, the Obama administration on December 29, 2016, expelled 35 Russian diplomats. One day later, Trump praised President Putin for not retaliating against the United States. At President Trump's first press conference, he decried as "fake news" reports of a secret Russian dossier containing compromising information about him. The dossier's contents, disclosed on the BuzzFeed website, have yet to be reliably verified (Bensinger, Elder, and Schoofs 2017).

A major controversy erupted on February 13 when National Security Advisor Mike Flynn resigned amid allegations that he made improper overtures to Russian ambassador Sergei Kislyak before Trump took office. The firing offense, however, was that he had misled Vice President Pence on the nature of those contacts. On March 2, Attorney General Jeff Sessions recused himself from any role in investigating Russian activity. He did this in response to reports that he had twice met with Ambassador Kislyak, though Sessions indicated he had those meetings in his capacity as a senator. President Trump issued a stunning tweet on March 4 charging the Obama administration with wiretapping Trump Tower in Manhattan.

FBI Director James Comey, at a congressional hearing on March 20, indicated he had no evidence supporting Trump's tweet. Comey did, however, confirm that an active FBI investigation was examining links between the Russian government and Trump associates as part of a broader investigation of Russian interference in the election.

On May 9, Trump fired James Comey, creating great public controversy about the dismissal and the reasons for it. The firing was peremptory and surprised Washington. The public announcement fell upon Comey without prior warning while he was addressing Los Angeles FBI agents. He learned of his dismissal via television. The administration had no replacement for Comey ready. The White House press secretary Sean Spicer issued a statement claiming that "President Trump acted based on the clear recommendations of both Deputy Attorney General Rod Rosenstein and Attorney General Jeff Sessions" (Taylor 2017).

The president then contradicted this explanation in a media interview two days later. Trump indicated he intended to fire Comey regardless of the recommendation he received from Rosenstein and Sessions, stating, "I was going to fire regardless of the recommendation. . . . And in fact when I decided to just do it, I said to myself, I said you know, this Russia thing with Trump and Russia is a made-up story, it's an excuse by the Democrats for having lost an election that they should have won" (Hains 2017). Trump's statements fueled speculation that he may have engaged in obstruction of justice by impeding the FBI Russia investigation. Yet Trump in the interview indicated he wanted that investigation "speeded up" because it was damaging his presidency. His statements contradicted the earlier White House statements about the decision, damaging the credibility of his press secretary.

The next day, Trump aggravated the controversy with an aggressive tweet: "James Comey better hope there are no 'tapes' of our conversations before he starts leaking to the press!" This led to a flurry of media speculations about whether a White House taping system exists. With this tweet and the firing of Comey, Trump unwittingly encouraged comparisons between this incident and the "Saturday night massacre" of 1973 when an embattled Richard Nixon fired Archibald Cox, the Watergate special prosecutor, and his attorney general and deputy attorney general, both of whom refused to fire Cox. Democrats were quick to issue Watergate analogies, terming Trump "Nixonian" (Watson 2017).

Reports then surfaced that Trump asked Comey in a private meeting to end an investigation into fired National Security Advisor Mike Flynn's ties with Russia (Barrett, Nakashima, and Zapotosky 2017). Comey himself had initiated some of these leaks. This again raised the specter of a possible obstruction of justice by Trump in attempting to abort an ongoing FBI investigation. The president, however, has legal authority to fire an FBI director and to direct him in his duties.

Was this another Watergate? Bob Woodward, a *Washington Post* reporter who broke that story, thought not: "This is not yet Watergate—no clear crime. . . . Now that doesn't mean, you know, that we know where this is going. There's a tremendous amount of smoke." Woodward noted that Watergate involved a former White House counsel, John Dean, describing how Nixon had "corruptly and illegally led the obstruction of justice," but "there is no evidence at this point that President Trump is involved in collusion here" (Fox News 2017).

On May 17, a week after Comey's firing, Deputy Attorney General Ron Rosenstein appointed a special council with broad authority to investigate Russian influence in the 2016 election, Trump campaign, and Trump administration. Robert Mueller, a former FBI director with a reputation for integrity, took charge of the investigation as special counsel. He was empowered to issue subpoenas and to recommend charges, though criminal charges cannot be filed against a current president. Trump responded by tweet that he was the target of a "witch hunt" by his political opponents.

By this time, multiple congressional committees—House Intelligence, Senate Intelligence, House Oversight, and Senate Judiciary Subcommittee on Crime and Terrorism—were investigating the Russian role in the 2016 election and, by implication, in the Trump transition and administration (LoBianco 2017). On June 8, former FBI director James Comey testified before the Senate Intelligence Committee.

Comey charged that Trump's assertions that the FBI was poorly led and in disarray as "lies, plain and simple." He further stated, "It's my judgment that I was fired because of the Russia investigation. I was fired in some way to change, or the endeavor was to change, the way the Russia investigation was being conducted." He indicated that Trump, at a private dinner on January 27, had stated to him, "I need loyalty." The president at a private meeting on February 14 had said to him regarding the FBI investigation of Mike Flynn, "I hope you can see your way clear to letting this go, to letting Flynn go. He is a good guy. I hope you can let this go." The president, however, told Comey in a subsequent phone call "that if there were some 'satellite' associates of his who did something wrong, it would be good to find that out" (CNN 2017).

Was this obstruction of justice? That is in the eye of the beholder. It may signal such intent, but it was not accompanied by direct orders or, apparently, a series of subsequent actions to obstruct the ongoing FBI investigation. Further, the president had the legal right to order an investigation closed and probably cannot be prosecuted for criminal offenses, though Trump's behavior might encourage charges of impeachment for "high crimes and misdemeanors." Impeachment is a political process, not required to apply only to violations of the law. More conclusive evidence about the possible obstruction charge was not forthcoming at the time.

Comey, however, did corroborate Trump's previous claim that Comey had three times told Trump that he was not under investigation by the FBI. He also stated, "There have been many, many stories based on—well, lots of stuff, but about Russia that are dead wrong." Specifically, he stated in reference to a February 14 *New York Times* story asserting that Trump's campaign and members of his administration had been in regular contact with Russian intelligence officials, "in the main it was not true." The night before Comey's testimony, CNN had claimed that Comey would contradict Trump's assertion that he had been told three times by Comey that he was not under investigation. The next day, the network retracted the false story (Easley 2017).

Trump in response claimed, via tweet, "total vindication" from Comey's testimony, although his lawyer, Mark Kasowitz, indicated the administration was contemplating legal action against Comey for leaking information to the media. The next day Trump told the press he was willing to testify under oath that he did not ask for "loyalty" or ask Comey to drop the Flynn investigation (Borchers 2017). That future possibility will be up to the ongoing investigation by Special Counsel Robert Mueller.

Neither Trump nor Comey enhanced their reputations during this episode. Trump's behavior was unpresidential and threatened to get him into further legal problems. The president is unlikely to prepare adequately, and thus testimony under oath could trap him in a number of contradictory statements (Allen 2017). Comey's leaks of memos detailing his meetings with Trump were unauthorized disclosures of information vital to an ongoing investigation by Special Counsel Mueller. Trump's lawyers accused Comey of illegal leaks. George Washington law professor Jonathan Turley summarized it well: "The greatest irony is that Trump succeeded in baiting Comey to a degree that even Trump could not have imagined. After calling Comey a 'showboat' and poor director, Comey proceeded to commit an unethical and unprofessional act in leaking damaging memos against Trump" (Turley 2017).

The Russia controversy flared again in June 2017 with the disclosure that Donald Trump Jr. had a meeting with a Russian lawyer at Trump Tower during the presidential campaign. Trump Jr. agreed to a meeting at the behest of acquaintance and music promoter Bob Goldstone, who promised that a Russian "government attorney" had compromising information regarding Hillary Clinton. Trump Jr. responded in an email that "if it's what you say, I love it," and he agreed to a meeting. The meeting on June 9, 2016, included Trump Jr., campaign director Paul Manafort, and Jared Kushner along with Russian attorney Natalia Veselnitskaya and three other Russians.

Though Veselnitskaya reportedly began the meeting with a general mention of overseas donations to the Clinton campaign, most of the 20-minute meeting, according to Kushner and Trump Jr., concerned changing US policy on Russian adoptions. Kushner later testified before a Senate committee that he found the meeting of no interest and texted an assistant to call him so he could leave immediately. His testimony revealed few contacts with Russians; Kushner asserted there was never any campaign collusion with Russians. Trump Jr. termed the encounter a "nothing meeting" and claimed no further contact with any of the Russians (Kushner 2017; Kinery 2017).

At best this incident revealed very bad judgment by Donald Trump Jr. and showcased his inexperience and questionable competence as a campaign operative. More experienced campaign consultants indicated they would never have met with any Russian officials in such a situation. The striking aspect of the incident was Trump Jr.'s desire to potentially collude with Russians and ignorance of the ethical dangers in such a course of action. The revelation gave new impetus to the Trump-Russia scandal narrative, which seemed destined for a long life.

After Trump's first six months in office, the three questions at the heart of the Russia probe remain unresolved, perhaps to be answered by Robert Mueller's investigation. The extent of Russian election interference in 2016 is not yet known. The relations between Russian interests and the Trump campaign, transition, and administration remain unclear. Trump's personal role with Russians during this time, despite his denials, has yet to be clarified. Speculation spiked again with the disclosure that former campaign manager Paul Manafort's home had received an FBI dawn raid with a "no knock" warrant on July 26. Like the lengthy Whitewater investigation during Bill Clinton's presidency, the Russia inquiry seems likely to extend far into Trump's tenure in the White House.

TRUMP'S EARLY RECORD WITH THE PRESIDENCY

Donald Trump's initial months in the presidency have produced much sound and fury and a flurry of executive orders and memoranda changing previous policies. His direction of foreign policy, examined in detail in another chapter, has been controversial. It's important to note that these Trump initiatives are easily overturned by a presidential successor. Much scarcer are important changes in law passed by Trump's Republican Congress.

Trump's three White House predecessors—Bill Clinton, George W. Bush, and Barack Obama—all issued executive orders and memoranda changing previous policies, much like Trump. These can be and have been steadily overturned by rival successors. Executive orders and memoranda in areas such as energy, environment, and international funding of abortions have flip-flopped over the years. Clinton and Bush overturned policies of their GOP predecessors and Trump and Bush overturned Democratic policies. Trump's record with these actions is unexceptional. Yet because so much of Obama's legacy was wrapped up in executive orders and memoranda, Trump has a much richer array of targets than did his predecessors.

His three predecessors, who, like Trump, had supportive partisan Congresses during their early months in office, could all claim early and important legislative achievements. By August of his first term, Clinton had signed into law the Family and Medical Leave Act, the Motor Voter Registration Act, and an ambitious deficit reduction plan. George W. Bush had signed a massive $1.35 trillion tax cut into law. Barack Obama likewise signed the Lilly Ledbetter Fair Pay Act and a large $831 billion Economic Recovery Act into law and had gained Senate approval of Sonya Sotomayor as a Supreme Court justice. Aside from his successful appointment of Neil Gorsuch to the Supreme Court, Trump had no comparable legislative accomplishments on his record.

Richard Neustadt, an eminent presidential scholar, argued that the presidency is a "weak" institution since so much presidential success depends on the consent of other governmental and nongovernmental actors (Neustadt 1990, ix–x). It is up to the president to engage in "self-help" because no one shares the president's perspective. The best form of self-help, Neustadt argues, is to think of power "prospectively" and "husband" one's power prospects because that power will be needed and used in the future (1990, xi). Early blunders, Neustadt argued, are particularly costly for a president: "A blunder is worse than a crime" (1990, xvi).

Presidential scholar George C. Edwards III notes that the current era of the "permanent campaign" for partisan advantage between elections makes presidential governance difficult: "In sum, the tendencies of the permanent campaign are for civility to lose out to conflict, compromise to deadlock, deliberation to sound bites and legislative product to campaign issue" (Edwards 2016, 211). New administrations start with the "arrogance of ignorance" and frequently make mistakes. Attempts by presidents to dominate government thus are not successful: "The political system is too complicated, power is too decentralized, and interests are too diverse for one person, no matter how extraordinary, to dominate" (203). A better approach, he argues, is for a president to pursue a strategy of "quiet negotiation" (211).

Trump's early record is a testament to how weak the presidency can be if the office is not handled well initially by its occupant. Trump's approach to the presidency so far is pretty much the opposite of that counseled by Neustadt and Edwards. Trump embraces the "permanent campaign" in office, trafficking in and relishing conflict in his public statements and personal tweets. He and his White House staff have very limited experience with Washington governance. Predictable results are errors due to arrogance and ignorance. Contradictory statements and factual errors emerge from the White House with unsettling frequency.

Trump's personality seeks the domination of others, which is no recipe for success in a system of separated powers. Quiet negotiation—indeed, any form of quiet—is seldom the president's approach to his job. Trump and his White House focus daily on battles with political opponents, with little apparent consideration of the president's future power prospects.

This approach is particularly unhelpful in an era of "revelation, investigation and prosecution" as defined by political scientists Benjamin Ginsberg and Martin Shefter: "Taken together, the expanded political roles of the national news media and the federal judiciary have given rise to a major new weapon of political combat: revelation, investigation and prosecution. The acronym for this, RIP, forms a fitting political epitaph for the public officials who have become its targets" (Ginsberg and Shefter 2002, 36–37). This phenomenon, now focused on Trump, can have ominous systemic consequences: "Electoral verdicts can now be reversed outside the electoral arena. . . . Today elected officials subjected to RIP attacks often find that their poll standings (today's substitute for an organized popular base) can evaporate overnight and their capacity to govern disappear with them" (213). By persisting in his Twitter battles, Trump risks an RIP fate that effectively overturns his election. Several media, governmental, and judicial rivals are challenging his hold on the presidency.

Let's finally return to those aspects of the presidency noted at the beginning of this chapter. Trump's daily focus on colorful conflicts displaces the quiet negotiations that can make the presidency operate effectively. The National Security Council, Defense, and State Departments have long functioned on the basis of quiet negotiation. The Office of Management and Budget, handling the president's budget proposal and legislative program, focuses on consultations with Congress often far from the media spotlight. Cabinet officers likewise go about their business without seeking the bright light of constant publicity. President Trump, with his outsized media presence and penchant for constant quarrels, often removes himself from the more constructive routines of government. As Neustadt and Edwards indicate, there's a big price to be paid for that.

WORKS CITED

ABC News. "A Look at Trump's Cabinet Picks." March 3, 2017. http://abcnews .go.com/Politics/trump-cabinet/story?id=43478002 (accessed June 8, 2017).

Allen, Mike. "Axios AM: 1 Big Thing: Trump's Bad Idea." June 10, 2017. https:// www.axios.com/axios-am-2438501237.html?utm_source=newsletter&utm _medium=email&utm_campaign=newsletter_axiosam&stream=top-stories (accessed June 11, 2017).

Barnes, Robert. "Supreme Court Allows Trump Refugee Ban but Backs Broader Exemptions for Relatives." *Washington Post*. July 19, 2017. https://www.washing tonpost.com/politics/courts_law/supreme-court-allows-trump-travel-ban -enforcement-but-says-it-must-allow-broader-exemptions-for-relatives/20 17/07/19/6945e01e-6bf8-11e7-96ab-5f38140b38cc_story.html?utm_term= .c2b64a369e3a (accessed July 24, 2017).

Barrett, Devlin, Ellen Nakashima, and Matt Zapotosky. "Notes by FBI Director Comey Say Trump Pressured Him to End Flynn Probe." *Washington Post*. May 16, 2017. https://www.washingtonpost.com/world/national-security/notes -made-by-former-fbi-director-comey-say-trump-pressured-him-to-end-flynn -probe/2017/05/16/52351a38-3a80-11e7-9e48-c4f199710b69_story.html?utm_ term=.9a946763674b (accessed August 21, 2017).

Bensinger, Ken, Miriam Elder, and Mark Schoofs. "These Reports Allege Trump Has Deep Ties to Russia." BuzzFeed News. January 10, 2017. https:// www.buzzfeed.com/kenbensinger/these-reports-allege-trump-has-deep-ties-to -russia?utm_term=.xfr216XNN#.elE9WqEPP (accessed June 11, 2017).

Borchers, Callum. "Everything President Trump Has Said about Comey's Testimony, Ranked." June 9, 2017. https://www.washingtonpost.com/news/the-fix/wp/2017/06/09/everything-president-trump-has-said-about-comeys-testimony-ranked/?utm_term=.6260ed113de0 (accessed June 11, 2017).

Bui, Quoctrung, Claire Cain Miller, and Kevin Quealy. "Is the Trump Presidency Getting More Normal? Experts Rate 28 Events." *New York Times.* May 3, 2017. https://www.nytimes.com/interactive/2017/05/03/upshot/has-the-trump-presidency-gotten-more-normal-an-expert-panel-rates-28-events.html?rref=collection%2Fsectioncollection%2Fupshot&action=click&contentCollection=upshot&region=rank&module=package&version=highlights&contentPlacement=1&pgtype=sectionfront&_r=1 (accessed June 8, 2017).

CBC News. "Russia and the Trump Administration: A Timeline." June 7, 2017. http://www.cbc.ca/news/world/trump-russia-investigations-comey-putin-1.4149266 (accessed June 9, 2017).

Clark, Charles S. "No, the Trump Transition Is Not Far Behind That of Previous Presidents." *Government Executive.* January 24, 2017. http://www.govexec.com/management/2017/01/no-trump-transition-not-far-behind-previous-presidents/134830/ (accessed June 8, 2017).

CNN. "Read: James Comey's Prepared Testimony." June 8, 2017. http://www.cnn.com/2017/06/07/politics/james-comey-memos-testimony/index.html (accessed June 10, 2017).

Davis, Aaron C. "D.C. and Maryland Sue President Trump, Citing Breach of Constitutional Oath." *Washington Post.* June 12, 2017. https://www.washingtonpost.com/local/dc-politics/dc-and-maryland-to-sue-president-trump-alleging-breach-of-constitutional-oath/2017/06/11/0059e1f0-4f19-11e7-91eb-9611861a988f_story.html?utm_term=.5bc5f7c5e26d (accessed June 13, 2017).

DeCosta-Klipa, Nik. "Remember Trump's 100 Day Plan? Here's What He Has and Hasn't Done." Boston.com. April 27, 2017. www.boston.com/news/politics/2017/04/27/remember-trumps-100-day-plan-heres-what-he-has-and-hasnt-done (accessed June 9, 2017).

Dilanian, Ken, and Alexandra Jaffe. "Trump Transition Shake-Up Part of 'Stalinesque Purge' of Christie Loyalists." *NBC News.* November 15, 2016. http://www.nbcnews.com/politics/2016-election/trump-transition-shake-part-stalinesque-purge-christie-loyalists-n684081 (accessed August 21, 2017).

"Donald Trump's Contract with the American Voter." 2016. https://assets.donaldjtrump.com/_landings/contract/O-TRU-102316-Contractv02.pdf (accessed August 21, 2017).

Easley, Jonathan. "Comey Rips Media for 'Dead Wrong' Russia Stories." *The Hill.* June 8, 2017. http://thehill.com/policy/national-security/336960-comey-rips-media-for-dead-wrong-russia-stories (accessed June 11, 2017).

Edwards, George C., III. *Predicting the Presidency: The Potential of Persuasive Leadership.* Princeton, NJ: Princeton University Press, 2016.

Forbes. "The Definitive Net Worth of Donald Trump." February 28, 2017. https://www.forbes.com/donald-trump/#6efe16102899 (accessed June 8, 2017).

Fox News. "Woodward on Trump Firing Comey: 'This Is Not Yet Watergate.'" May 4, 2017. http://www.foxnews.com/politics/2017/05/14/woodward-on-trump-russia-this-is-not-yet-watergate.html (accessed June 11, 2017).

Frady, Marshall. "The Big Guy." *New York Review of Books.* November 1, 2002. http://www.nybooks.com/articles/2002/11/07/the-big-guy/ (accessed June 8, 2017).

Gilbert, Lisa. "We the People Do Care about Trump's Taxes." CNN. April 14, 2017. http://www.cnn.com/2017/04/14/opinions/people-do-care-trump-taxes-opinion-gilbert/index.html (accessed June 9, 2017).

Ginsberg, Benjamin, and Martin Shefter. *Politics by Other Means: Politicians, Prosecutors, and the Press from Watergate to Whitewater.* New York: Norton, 2002.

Gold, Matea. "White House Grants Ethics Waivers to 17 Appointees, Including Four Former Lobbyists." *Washington Post.* May 31, 2017. https://www.washingtonpost.com/news/post-politics/wp/2017/05/31/white-house-grants-ethics-waivers-to-17-appointees-including-four-former-lobbyists/?utm_term=.f59d4ca8b2b9 (accessed June 9, 2017).

Gold, Matea, and Juliet Eilperin. "Limited Ethics Waivers Reflect New Freedom for Lobbyists to Join Government." *Washington Post.* June 7, 2017. https://www.washingtonpost.com/politics/limited-ethics-waivers-reflect-new-freedom-for-former-lobbyists-to-join-government/2017/06/07/f02bbaf0-4b95-11e7-a186-60c031eab644_story.html?utm_term=.4116491ee128&wpisrc=nl_daily202&wpmm=1 (accessed June 9, 2017).

Greenwood, Max. "Trump Gives Commanders New Powers to Launch Military Strikes: Report." *The Hill.* March 3, 2017. http://thehill.com/policy/defense/322259-trump-granted-commanders-expanded-authority-to-order-military-action-report (accessed June 8, 2017).

Hains, Tim. "President Trump's Full Interview with Lester Holt: The Firing of James Comey." RealClearPolitics. May 11, 2017. https://www.realclearpolitics.com/video/2017/05/11/president_trumps_full_interview_with_lester_holt.html (accessed June 11, 2017).

Harwell, Drew. "Trump Outlines Plan to Shift Assets, Give Up His Management Company." *Washington Post.* January 11, 2017. https://www.washingtonpost.com/politics/trump-outlines-plan-to-shift-assets-give-up-management-of-his-company/2017/01/11/8c7527d8-d801-11e6-b8b2-cb5164beba6b_story.html?utm_term=.80cb5e055183 (accessed June 8, 2017).

Holmes, Jack. "A Definitive Timeline of Donald Trump's Many Excuses about His Taxes." *Esquire.* January 23, 2017. http://www.esquire.com/news-politics/videos/a52466/donald-trump-tax-returns-timeline/ (accessed June 9, 2017).

Hopkins, Christopher Dean. "U.S. Ethics Official: Trump's Divestiture Is Hard, Pricey and Essential." Minnesota Public Radio. January 12, 2017. http://www.npr.org/sections/thetwo-way/2017/01/12/509421108/u-s-ethics-official-trumps-divestiture-is-hard-pricy-and-essential (accessed June 8, 2017).

Keegan, Michael J. "Perspectives on Presidential Transitions: How George W. Bush and Barack Obama Managed a Transfer of Power." IBM Center for the Business of Government. December 1, 2015. http://www.businessofgovernment.org/blog/business-government/perspective-presidential-transitions-how-george-w-bush-and-barack-obama-man (accessed June 8, 2017).

Kinery, Emma. "Timeline: Donald Trump Jr.'s Interactions with Kremlin-linked Lawyer." *USA Today*. July 11, 2017. https://www.usatoday.com/story/news/politics/2017/07/11/timeline-donald-trump-jr-interactions-kremlin-linked-lawyer/467634001/ (accessed July 23, 2017).

Kopan, Tal. "Trump Administration Lags in Filling Key Posts." CNN. February 17, 2017. http://www.cnn.com/2017/02/17/politics/donald-trump-administration-slow-appointments/index.html (accessed June 8, 2017).

Kramer, Andrew E., Mike McIntire, and Barry Meier. "Secret Ledger in Ukraine Lists Cash for Donald Trump's Campaign Chief." *New York Times*. August 14, 2016. https://www.nytimes.com/2016/08/15/us/politics/paul-manafort-ukraine-donald-trump.html?_r=0 (accessed June 10, 2017).

Kushner, Jared. "Statement of Jared C. Kushner to Congressional Committees." July 24, 2017. https://www.documentcloud.org/documents/3899497-Jared-Kushner-July-24-Statement-to-Congressional.html?utm_campaign=SocialFlow&utm_source=Twitter&utm_medium=AP (accessed July 24, 2017).

LoBianco, Tom. "The 4 Russian Investigations in Congress, Explained." April 25, 2017. http://www.cnn.com/2017/04/25/politics/congress-russia-investigations/index.html (accessed June 11, 2017).

McAdams, Dan P. "The Mind of Donald Trump." *The Atlantic*. June 2016. https://www.theatlantic.com/magazine/archive/2016/06/the-mind-of-donald-trump/480771/ (accessed August 21, 2017).

Mindock, Clark. "Russian Hackers Tried to Hack US Voting Software Days before Election, Leaked NSA Document Suggests." *Independent*. June 5, 2017. http://www.independent.co.uk/news/world/americas/us-politics/russian-hack-us-election-voting-software-leaked-nsa-document-a7774591.html (accessed June 11, 2017).

Neustadt, Richard E. *Presidential Power and the Modern Presidents*. New York: Free Press, 1990.

Newswise. "Foremost Presidential Transition Expert Talks Trump." November 14, 2016. http://www.newswise.com/articles/foremost-presidential-transitions-expert-talks-trump (accessed June 8, 2017).

Northam, Jackie, and Marilyn Geewax. "Ivanka Trump's Move to the White House Raises Questions about Ethics." *National Public Radio*. March 21,

2017. http://www.npr.org/sections/thetwo-way/2017/03/21/520965076/ivanka-trumps-move-to-the-white-house-raises-questions-about-ethics (accessed August 21, 2017).

Parker, Ashley. "Snubs and Slights Are Part of the Job in Trump's White House." *Washington Post.* May 29, 2017. https://www.washingtonpost.com/politics/snubs-and-slights-are-part-of-the-job-in-trumps-white-house/2017/05/29/f5c9d5c0-417a-11e7-9869-bac8b446820a_story.html?utm_term=.3c7461aee973 (accessed June 8, 2017).

Pramuk, Jacob. "Trump Explains Why He Ousted Comey Quickly—But Waited to Fire Flynn." CNBC. May 11, 2017. http://www.cnbc.com/2017/05/11/trump-explains-why-he-ousted-comey-quickly-but-waited-to-fire-flynn.html (accessed June 8, 2017).

Restuccia, Andrew, and Nancy Cook. "Trump Transition Team Pulls Out the Stops." *Politico.* November 3, 2016. http://www.politico.com/story/2016/11/trump-transition-team-pulls-out-the-stops-230666 (accessed August 21, 2017).

Reuters Staff. "U.S. Intel Report Identifies Russians Who Gave Emails to Wikileaks." *Reuters.* January 5, 2017. http://www.reuters.com/article/us-usa-russia-cyber-celebrate-idUSKBN14P2NI (accessed August 21, 2017).

Roff, Peter. "Down the Tax Return Rabbit Hole." *US News and World Report.* March 15, 2017. www.usnews.com/opinion/thomas-jefferson-street/articles/2017-03-15/rachel-maddow-embarrassed-herself-democrats-on-donald-trumps-tax-returns (accessed June 9, 2017).

Rossiter, Clinton. *The American Presidency.* New York: Harcourt Brace, 1956.

Rubenzer, Steven J., and Thomas R. Faschingbauer. *Personality, Character and Leadership in the White House: Psychologists Assess the Presidents.* Washington, DC: Brassey's, 2004.

Saletan, William. "The White House Is Lying about Comey." *Slate.* May 10, 2017. http://www.slate.com/articles/news_and_politics/politics/2017/05/the_white_house_story_on_comey_s_firing_is_falling_apart.html (accessed June 8, 2017).

Scherer, Michael, and Zeke J. Miller. "Donald Trump after Hours." *Time.* May 11, 2017. http://time.com/donald-trump-after-hours/ (accessed June 8, 2017).

Schouten, Fredrika. "Donald Trump's Presidency Raises Novel Ethics Questions." *USA Today.* October 6, 2015. https://www.usatoday.com/story/news/politics/elections/2015/10/06/donald-trump-campaign-ethics-questions/73409764/ (accessed June 8, 2017).

Taylor, Jessica. "President Trump Fires FBI Director James Comey." Minnesota Public Radio. May 9, 2017. http://www.npr.org/2017/05/09/527663050/president-trump-fires-fbi-director-james-comey (accessed June 11, 2017).

Trump, Donald J. *Trump: The Art of the Deal.* New York: Random House, 1987.

Turley, Jonathan. "The Damaging Case against James Comey." *The Hill.* June 9, 2017. http://thehill.com/blogs/pundits-blog/the-administration/337160-opinion-the-damaging-case-against-james-comey (accessed June 11, 2017).

Washington Post. "Fact Checker: In 181 Days, President Trump Has Made 836 False and Misleading Claims." July 24, 2017a. https://www.washingtonpost .com/graphics/politics/trump-claims-database/?utm_term=.bcc039c5111a (accessed July 24, 2017).

Washington Post. "Tracking How Many Key Positions Trump Has Filled So Far." June 9, 2017b. https://www.washingtonpost.com/graphics/politics/trump -administration-appointee-tracker/database/ (accessed July 24, 2017).

Watson, Kathryn. "Democrats Compare Trump's Firing of Comey to Nixon and Watergate." CBS News. May 9, 2017. http://www.cbsnews.com/news/ democrats-compare-trumps-firing-of-comey-to-nixon-and-watergate/ (accessed June 11, 2017).

Yu, Roger. "Trump Signs Legislation to Scrap Dodd-Frank Rule on Oil Extraction." *USA Today.* February 14, 2017. https://www.usatoday.com/story/money /2017/02/14/trump-scraps-dodd-frank-rule-resource-extraction-disclosure/ 97912600/ (accessed June 9, 2017).

Zarroli, Jim. "Trump Relatives' Potential White House Roles Could Test Anti-Nepotism Law." National Public Radio. January 5, 2017. http://www.npr.org/ 2017/01/05/508382236/trump-relatives-potential-white-house-roles-could-test -anti-nepotism-law (accessed June 9, 2017).

3

Trump and Congress

@realDonaldTrump
We will immediately repeal and replace ObamaCare—and nobody can
do that like me. We will save $'s and have much better healthcare!
(5:15:34 p.m., February 9, 2016)

@realDonaldTrump
The U.S. Senate should switch to 51 votes, immediately, and get
Healthcare and TAX CUTS approved, fast and easy. Dems would do
it, no doubt!
(8:59:28 a.m., May 30, 2017)

WHAT THE CONSTITUTION SEPARATES

Many studies of the presidency present a picture of an executive branch
playing a leading role in policymaking. Presidents set agendas, direct
national attention, and guide Congress to act. This perception of the presidency has been especially common in the decades following the active
and assertive presidency of Franklin Roosevelt. Reality paints a far less
impressive picture of the unilateral powers of the president. Though the
power of the presidency has expanded significantly, the executive branch
remains as only one player in a much larger system. Though presidents
may enjoy rather significant power to determine US foreign policy,
meaningful domestic policy requires legislation, and that requires the

cooperation of Congress. As the era of divided government emerged in the late 1960s, many scholars looked to the influence of party as an explanation for the breakdown in cooperation between presidents and Congress. But recent periods of unified government, including President Trump's first year in office, have reminded many of the warning offered by Richard Neustadt in his classic work on presidential power—"What the constitution separates our political parties do not combine" (1991, 29). Neustadt meant that the divisions and rivalries inherent in our system of "separate institutions sharing power" cannot be bridged easily. Though presidents and a congressional majority may share party affiliation, they are often motivated by divergent interests and beholden to different electorates and different electoral calendars and calculations.

These differences, and the constitutional mandate of shared authority, all but guarantee a relationship between a president and Congress that will be challenging regardless of which party controls each. As outlined by Roger Davidson, successful presidents must persuade and bargain with Congress at all possible levels—from meetings with congressional leadership to one-on-one negotiations with individual members (Pfiffner and Davidson 2013). Failure to engage in such a manner risks failure of a president's agenda. Given the bully pulpit offered by the presidency, some presidents have opted for a strategy of "going public" in an effort to sway public opinion and influence Congress. Davidson warns that such a strategy should be used as a last resort only when more effective approaches have been tried. Though presidents may be tempted by the promises of public outreach, such approaches are fraught with limitations. Specifically, Davidson (302) warns public appeals may "raise expectations that cannot be filled, make inept appeals, lose control of the issue, alienate legislators whose support is needed, or put forward hastily conceived proposals." The reality of Davidson's words can be seen in the early days of the Trump presidency.

The fate of Trump's ambitious legislative agenda and confirmations of his political and judicial appointees will be determined by his relationship with Congress. Much like Obama in 2009, Trump will preside over a unified federal government. Democrats rallied around President Obama as Republicans vowed to make him a one-term president. Have Republicans rallied around Trump? Have Democrats sought out common ground with Trump or have they adopted the Republican strategy against Obama? Vice President Mike Pence was initially viewed as a powerful liaison between the White House and Congress, but it's unclear just how much Pence has been able to deliver.

TRUMP'S POLITICAL CAPITAL

Political scientist James Thurber (2017) identifies three factors that are crucial to a president's likelihood of success: a clear popular vote advantage, a decisive Electoral College victory, and a Congress clearly controlled by allies of the newly elected president (4). According to Thurber, every minority president, save for one, has had at least one of those factors working in his favor at the time of his inauguration. The exception was George W. Bush in January 2001. This could be troubling for Trump as he and Bush have something in common. Though many presidents have been elected without a majority of the popular vote, very few have been elected without a plurality of the popular vote. So being a "minority president" is neither uncommon nor an indication of success or failure. But of the 39 men elected president since the popular vote became widespread in the 1830s, only four became president having failed to win the popular vote—Rutherford B. Hayes, William Henry Harrison, George W. Bush, and Donald J. Trump. Given the myriad changes in American politics and presidential and congressional relations little can be gleaned from comparing Trump to either Hayes or Harrison, so the initial experiences of George W. Bush may be more informative.

Unlike most presidents, George W. Bush was met with none of the three crucial factors identified by Thurber. Bush had lost the popular vote, he had won the narrowest of Electoral College victories, and he was met with a minimal 10-seat majority in the House and 50–50 tie in the Senate. It was the tie-breaking vote of his vice president, Dick Cheney, that delivered the slimmest of Senate majorities. Like many minority presidents, Bush had pledged to reach out to Democrats and to govern in a bipartisan manner. Like Bush, Trump promised in the hours after his victory to be a president to all Americans and to work together with Democrats in an effort to move the nation forward.

Bush's pledge of bipartisanship was short lived, and the pursuit of a decidedly conservative agenda resulted in the defection of a Republican senator and the loss of the Senate. Bush's bare Senate majority became a slight but significant Democratic majority only 6 months into his first term. This created a major roadblock for President Bush's legislative priorities during his first year in office—until serious world events intervened in September 2001.

A cursory review suggests that Trump may enjoy advantages that George W. Bush did not. Though Trump lost the popular vote to Hillary

Clinton, he did secure a seemingly comfortable Electoral College victory, and his party was in clear control of Congress. When Trump was sworn in as the forty-fifth president of the United States, he inherited something quite rare for newly elected Republican presidents—true unified control of government. Trump's Republican Party held a clear 47-seat majority in the United States House of Representatives and a narrow, but clear, two-seat majority in the US Senate. Though unified control of government was once the norm in American politics, it has become increasingly rare since the late 1960s. Between 1901 and 1968 there was unified control of government during 27 of the 34 Congresses seated over that time. Since 1968, unified government has been present for only 7 of 25 Congresses. All told, Trump appeared to enter the White House with two out of the three crucial factors identified by Thurber on his side. Unfortunately for Trump, the reality of those supposed advantages may be far less beneficial to his agenda.

Though Trump received the most Electoral College votes of any Republican victor since George H. W. Bush in 1992, his margin was far from historic. Of the 54 presidential elections held since 1804, Trump's share of the electoral vote ranked 44th in size (Silver 2016). In other words, only 10 presidential elections have produced a winner with a smaller share of the electoral vote. Though Republicans enjoy a House majority as large as any they've had since 1947, the slenderness of the Senate majority, coupled with intense partisan polarizations and divisions among congressional Republicans regarding President Trump's candidacy and agenda, limits Trump's ability to count on those majorities. Finally, the influence of Trump's popular vote loss cannot be understated. George W. Bush had lost the popular vote by just over 500,000 votes, or half of a percentage point, but Trump lost by nearly 3 million votes and two percentage points. Had 40,000 voters in Pennsylvania, Michigan, and Wisconsin decided to vote for Clinton instead of Trump, he would have lost the election. Trump entered office with the lowest approval rating of any president in the modern era (Gallup 2017). To quote Professor Josh Chafetz, "Trump came into office having lost the popular vote by quite a bit, with many of those who did vote for him having done so reluctantly, and his approval rating has been significantly underwater since the second week of his presidency. And he never had much support from GOP elites" (Chafetz 2017b). So Trump came to Washington with a political victory that shocked the world but produced virtually no political capital for the new president.

THE PRESIDENT'S LIMITED WINDOW
OF LEGISLATIVE OPPORTUNITY

Though Trump came to Washington with limited political capital, he did have an election victory under his belt and a unified (by party label) federal government. As such, there were expectations of legislative successes at least in those areas where the president's agenda overlapped with the legislative goals of congressional Republicans. Repeal of the Affordable Care Act as well as tax reform seemed like natural starting points of common ground (Binder in Thurber and Tana 2017). In late October 2016, candidate Trump signed a "Contract with the American Voter" in which he pledged to work with Congress to introduce and hold votes on 10 major pieces of legislation (Kelly and Sprunt 2016).

- Middle Class Tax Relief and Simplification Act: An economic plan designed to grow the economy 4 percent per year and create at least 25 million new jobs through massive tax reduction and simplification, in combination with trade reform, regulatory relief, and lifting the restrictions on American energy. The largest tax reductions are for the middle class. A middle-class family with 2 children will get a 35 percent tax cut. The current number of brackets will be reduced from 7 to 3, and tax forms will likewise be greatly simplified. The business rate will be lowered from 35 to 15 percent, and the trillions of dollars of American corporate money overseas can now be brought back at a 10 percent rate.
- End the Offshoring Act: Establishes tariffs to discourage companies from laying off their workers in order to relocate in other countries and ship their products back to the United States tax-free.
- American Energy and Infrastructure Act: Leverages public-private partnerships, and private investments through tax incentives, to spur $1 trillion in infrastructure investment over 10 years. It is revenue neutral.
- School Choice and Education Opportunity Act: Redirects education dollars to give parents the right to send their kids to the public, private, charter, magnet, religious, or home school of their choice. It ends common core and brings education supervision to local communities. It expands vocational and technical education and makes 2- and 4-year college more affordable.
- Repeal and Replace Obamacare Act: Fully repeals Obamacare and replaces it with health savings accounts, the ability to purchase health

insurance across state lines, and lets states manage Medicaid funds. Reforms will also include cutting the red tape at the FDA: there are more than 4,000 drugs awaiting approval, and we especially want to speed the approval of life-saving medications.

- Affordable Childcare and Eldercare Act: Allows Americans to deduct child care and elder care from their taxes, incentivizes employers to provide on-site child-care services, and creates tax-free dependent care savings accounts for both young and elderly dependents, with matching contributions for low-income families.
- End Illegal Immigration Act: Fully funds the construction of a wall on our southern border with the full understanding that the country Mexico will be reimbursing the United States for the full cost of such wall; establishes a 2-year mandatory minimum federal prison sentence for illegally reentering the United States after a previous deportation, and a 5-year mandatory minimum for illegally reentering for those with felony convictions, multiple misdemeanor convictions, or two or more prior deportations; reforms visa rules to enhance penalties for overstaying and to ensure that open jobs are offered to American workers first.
- Restoring Community Safety Act: Reduces surging crime, drugs, and violence by creating a Task Force on Violent Crime and increasing funding for programs that train and assist local police; increases resources for federal law enforcement agencies and federal prosecutors to dismantle criminal gangs and put violent offenders behind bars.
- Restoring National Security Act: Rebuilds our military by eliminating the defense sequester and expanding military investment; provides veterans with the ability to receive public VA treatment or attend the private doctor of their choice; protects our vital infrastructure from cyber-attack; establishes new screening procedures for immigration to ensure that those who are admitted to our country support our people and our values.
- Clean Up Corruption in Washington Act: Enacts new ethics reforms to drain the swamp and reduce the corrupting influence of special interests on our politics.

But major legislative victories were nowhere to be found during the early months of Trump's presidency. Though House Republicans had voted numerous times to repeal the Affordable Care Act, most of those votes were symbolic, as President Obama was certain to veto the measures.

Under unified control, however, any vote to end the Affordable Care Act would be very real for the millions of voters covered in some manner by the law.

In early March 2017, House leadership produced the American Health Care Act (AHCA) as the legislative vehicle by which the Affordable Care Act would be partially repealed and replaced. And the repeal and replace had to be partial because Republicans lacked the votes to overcome an expected Democratic filibuster in the Senate. As such, Republicans needed a bill that could proceed under a process known as "reconciliation," which eliminates the possibility of a filibuster in the Senate. The budget reconciliation process was created by the Budget Impoundment and Control Act of 1974 and sets forth a streamlined process for considering tax and revenue matters. As the process was created to streamline efforts to deal with budget deficits, Senate rules stipulate that reconciliation can only be used on budget-related matters. As a result, only some of the Affordable Care Act could be repealed via reconciliation. This meant that the AHCA was only the first of a necessary multipart approach to repealing and replacing the ACA. In order to meet reconciliation rules, the AHCA left much of the ACA's regulatory provisions intact. This meant that insurers would still be required to offer federally mandated minimum benefit options, children would still be permitted to remain on a parent's health plan until the age of 26, and participating insurers would be required to provide coverage to all regardless of any preexisting conditions. The AHCA did, however, eliminate most of the taxes contained in the ACA as well as the tax on individuals who opted to not buy health insurance. The Republican repeal bill curtailed the expansion of Medicaid, the public insurance program for low-income Americans.

A Congressional Budget Office review of the AHCA estimated that it would increase the number of uninsured Americans by 24 million by 2026 and result in substantial premium hikes for those with insurance (Kaplan and Pear 2017a). Though much of the increase in the number of uninsured resulted from the elimination of the unpopular individual mandate (meaning fewer people would choose to purchase coverage), that detail was largely overlooked in press accounts of the CBO report. A vote on the measure was expected to take place in late March 2017 but was ultimately scuttled when it became clear that the measure lacked the support of conservative House Republicans and could not secure enough votes to pass. Revisions made to the bill during the ensuing weeks attracted the support of conservatives but risked the support of moderates. The bill was amended to provide states with the freedom to request a waiver from the preexisting condition coverage requirements mandated by the ACA—provided the state established a high-risk coverage pool for folks who may lose coverage (Politifact 2017). Though still controversial, the amended AHCA passed the House by the slimmest of margins on May 4, 2017. But any celebration of that victory was short lived, as Senate Republicans made it clear that the House bill would not come up for consideration in the Senate; rather, the Senate would draft its own bill (Bryan 2017). In June 2017, nearly two months after the House had passed the AHCA, Republican senator Richard Burr stated that a health-care deal might not happen at all during the president's first year (Hellmann 2017).

During much of June 2017, Senate leadership worked behind closed doors to draft a version of the AHCA that could pass the Senate. Majority Leader Mitch McConnell received considerable criticism for the secretive manner in which the legislation was drafted, but McConnell wanted to avoid the very public process that had taken place in the House and had undermined public support for the law before it was ever introduced. When finally unveiled in late June, the Better Care Reconciliation Act (BCRA) lacked the 50 votes necessary to pass. As in the House, the Senate bill was opposed by conservatives who believed that it did not go far enough and by moderates who believed that it went too far (Lee, Fox, and Mattingly 2017). President Trump praised the bill but indicated that some negotiations remained before the bill would be finalized. Despite the closed-door proceedings and the presidential praise, the bill that emerged was little different from the House version that senators had described as dead on arrival and the president had described as "mean." Though the Senate bill retained more of the Affordable Care Act's subsidies for purchasing health insurance, a CBO analysis estimated that the legislation would result in 22 million more uninsured by 2026 than under current law and result in substantially higher premiums for older people—little different from the House version (Kaplan and Pear 2017b).

McConnell initially announced plans for a vote on the bill prior to the July 4 recess but scuttled those plans when it became obvious that the votes were not there to pass the bill (Beckwith, Elliott, and Abramson 2017). In an effort to boost the legislation's chances, President Trump invited all Senate Republicans to the White House. By the time of the White House meeting, 9 Republican senators had publicly announced opposition to the bill. McConnell could afford to lose no more than 2 Republican senators, assuming no Democratic support and a tie-breaking vote cast by Vice President Pence (Abramson 2017). In reality, Trump had been little involved in the Senate efforts to repeal the ACA because that was what Senate Republicans wanted. According to press accounts, the president wanted to be actively involved in whipping up support in the Senate (Everett and Dawsey 2017), but many senators and their senior staff believed that the prospects for success were greater the less Trump was involved (Merica, Fox, and Lee 2017). Following the White House meeting, Republican senators expressed optimism that the bill would pass. But in separate encounters Trump offered seemingly contradictory assurances to conservative and moderate critics of the legislation. Conservative senator Rand Paul, an advocate for repealing as much of the ACA as possible, held a one-on-one meeting with the president and announced that the president shared his belief that all concessions made thus far had been to moderate senators at the expense of a more substantive repeal effort. Moderate senator Susan Collins left the larger meeting with the president certain that he agreed that more of the ACA's coverage protections needed to be maintained (Everett and Dawsey 2017). At least one GOP senator offered that revisions to the Senate bill that would reduce costs overall while maintaining some protection for the working poor may be a way to satisfy the Paul and Collins factions within the party.

By engaging directly with the Senate negotiations over the bill, Trump raised the stakes regarding the bill's fate. Its failure would be viewed as a failure for Trump and his reputation as a deal maker. If the Senate did pass the legislation, his direct involvement would be viewed as a clear victory in unifying a very divided Republican caucus. Attendees at the White House meeting described Trump as engaged and acting very much as a chairman of the board, directing his organization, though not fully versed on the details (Everett and Dawsey 2017; Savransky 2017). The meeting added clarity to the Senate discussions, providing Republicans with a better understanding of where they agreed and where they still disagreed. Though Trump received generally high marks for the White House meeting with Senate Republicans, he noted during the meeting that it might be "OK" if the bill ultimately failed. Such a statement seemed to undermine the importance of repealing the ACA, one of Trump's biggest campaign promises.

As negotiation over the Senate bill continued, Trump again muddied the waters with a tweet suggesting that if the Senate were unable to pass the bill, it should simply vote to repeal the ACA in its entirety and then vote to replace it at a later date (Everett, Nelson, and Cancryn 2017). This was the strategy preferred by conservative Senate Republicans, and the tweet from the president may have weakened their willingness to compromise on the Senate's repeal and replace bill. Although the repeal bill could be accomplished via the streamlined budget reconciliation process, any subsequent replace bill would be subject to Democratic filibuster and would give Democrats an upper hand in negotiating any replacement bill. In the span of two weeks, the president went from boosting the chances of a Senate vote to repeal and replace the ACA to undermining those very chances. The challenges of such a lack of message discipline are discussed in greater detail in chapter 4.

Trump launched an "Infrastructure Week" public relations tour in early June, but the White House put forward no actual proposal or legislation and provided no time line for doing so (Bierman 2017). Unfortunately for the White House, former FBI Director James Comey testified before Congress during the heart of infrastructure week. The Comey hearing pushed the infrastructure discussion from the headlines—perhaps for the best. Though initial discussions suggested a $1 trillion infrastructure investment, deficit realities and pressure from conservatives resulted in the administration suggesting that the plan would be for $200 billion in new spending coupled with $800 billion in private investment spurred on by $140 billion in tax incentives and reduced red tape (O'Brien 2017). The Trump administration had yet to produce legislation or any policy details in the weeks and months that followed the early June push.

Piecemeal progress was made on the immigration front in July when the House passed one bill that would deny federal funds to so-called sanctuary cities that refuse to comply with federal immigration policy, and another bill would increase prison sentences for individuals who reenter the country illegally following deportation. The bills faced an uncertain future in the Senate, where they lacked broad-based support and were expected to face a Democratic filibuster should they be introduced. Eight Senate Democrats would need to join with all 52 Republicans to advance either bill (Huetteman and Kulish 2017).

In late July Mitch McConnell decided that the repeal and replace debate needed to be resolved. In a high-profile gamble, McConnell schedule a vote on a motion to proceed to consider the Senate's repeal and replace bill. Though this was merely a procedural vote to allow debate to begin, it was a crucial vote. If 51 senators opposed the motion to proceed, then there would be no consideration of a repeal and replace bill. McConnell understood that all 48 Democrats would oppose the motion, and at least two Republican moderates, Susan Collins of Maine and Lisa Murkowski of Arkansas, were "no" votes as well. McConnell needed every one of the remaining 50 GOP senators to vote in favor, thereby allowing Vice President Pence to cast the tie-breaking vote to proceed. In a dramatic development, Senator John McCain, who had been diagnosed with brain cancer only days before, announced that he would return to Washington, DC, and vote "yes" on the motion. McConnell's gamble had paid off. Repeal and replace would be debated on the Senate floor.

What followed, however, was a string of defeats as the main Republican repeal and replace measure was soundly beaten. As the end of the weeklong debate neared, Republican leadership rallied around a so-called skinny repeal of the Affordable Care Act (Hohmann 2017b). The scaled-back measure would eliminate the individual and employer mandates under the Affordable Care Act but leave much of the rest of the law intact. Insurers warned that elimination of the individual mandate would result in fewer young and healthy people buying insurance and result in higher premiums for everyone else, thus hastening the eventual demise of the Affordable Care Act. Just prior to 2 a.m. on Friday, July 28, the skinny repeal was defeated by a vote of 49 to 51. John McCain cast the deciding vote. Just moments before voting "no," McCain had been personally lobbied by Mike Pence and then by President Trump via cell phone. McCain knew that there were as many as 10 Republican senators who wanted to vote against the skinny repeal, but many feared political retribution from party leadership and party activists. McCain's "no" vote allowed them to vote "yes" (Pearlstein 2017). It's worth noting that there was never any love lost between John McCain and Donald Trump. During the campaign, Trump had dismissed the notion that McCain's six-year imprisonment in the Hanoi Hilton, the notorious North Vietnamese prison camp, earned him the designation of "war hero" (Shreckinger et al. 2015). Trump insisted instead that true heroes are the ones who don't get captured. Trump never apologized for the comment.

As spring yielded to summer and summer to fall in 2017, President Trump was faced with the very real possibility of no significant legislative accomplishments during his first year in office. A partial repeal and replacement of Obamacare passed the House in early May but died in the Senate in late July in a high-profile failure. Tax reform, comprehensive or otherwise, was stalled in both chambers, as many believed that a victorious health-care vote was needed to boost the chances of tax reform because the estimated budget savings from repealing the ACA would help to offset the costs of tax cuts contained in any reform package. A budget compromise hammered out by the House and Senate in the spring provided no funding for Trump's proposed border wall or for new investments in infrastructure and largely rebuked the deep spending cuts contained in Trump's first budget proposal (Caldwell 2017a; Taylor 2017). Near the end of July, the House approved a Defense Department funding bill that included $1.6 billion for the border wall, but its fate in the Senate was unclear. This is a troubling state of affairs for the president's legislative ambitions. If history is any guide, Trump's window of opportunity for meaningful legislative accomplishments is closing fast.

THE CRUCIAL FIRST YEARS

When unified government has existed in recent decades it has been more common during the first 2 years of a newly elected president's first term. As a result, the first two years in office have become a critical period during which presidents seek to maximize legislative accomplishments. In an era of intense partisan polarization, a newly elected president must rely on a high level of support in Congress from members of his/her own party and expect minimal cooperation from members of the opposition party.

Though many observers of American politics assume that there is greater legislative productivity under unified government, there is considerable evidence to the contrary. David Mayhew (2005), in his classic work *Divided We Govern*, examined the number of important laws passed by Congress between 1946 and 1990 and found that unified control of government was inconsequential to the success or failure of a president's legislative agenda. Further examination of legislation through 2014 yielded the same conclusion. So what does determine legislative success? Political scientist Keith Krehbiel offers that it boils down to the procedural powers held by the Congress and the president. As summarized by Sarah Binder in *Rivals for Power* (Thurber and Tama 2017), Krehbiel sees the veto and the filibuster as the crucial factors in a game of *pivotal politics*. The pivots points are determined by the two-thirds majority needed to override a presidential veto and the three-fifths majority required in the Senate to invoke cloture and end a filibuster. The only legislation that is likely to succeed, regardless of partisan control of government, is legislation that enjoys support at or beyond those pivot points. Under unified government, the cloture threshold becomes the key pivot as it measures the strength of the opposition party. Under divided government, the veto override threshold becomes the key pivot as it determines which branch has an upper hand in legislative negotiations.

Under this understanding, Bill Clinton and Barack Obama had legislatively productive first years not simply because of unified Democratic control of government, but because many of their legislative initiatives enjoyed support sufficient to overcome filibuster efforts in the Senate. When Republicans reclaimed control of the House and the Senate following the 2014 midterm elections, they used their majority to block Obama's agenda, but President Obama was then able to block the GOP's legislative agenda because the party lacked the votes to override a veto. Bill Clinton survived the loss of the congressional majority after the 1994 midterm elections by adopting broadly popular policy items that enjoyed support beyond the pivot points. President George W. Bush struggled in his first year in office because Democrats had well beyond the 41 votes necessary to sustain a filibuster in the 50–50 Senate. Bush was able to enact major tax reform only because Senate budget reconciliation rules deprived Democrats of the ability to filibuster.

Donald Trump's difficulties thus far are at least partially the result of his legislative priorities occupying positions somewhere outside of the cloture pivot point—his priorities lack supermajority support and therefore languish. Krehbiel's theory of pivotal politics makes clear why Republicans cannot undertake a straightforward repeal and replace legislative approach to deal with the Affordable Care Act. Any such approach would be filibustered in the Senate, where Republicans lack the votes required to invoke cloture. Instead, the party must pursue the rather messy and piecemeal approach described in this chapter so that it can use the reconciliation process and bypass the cloture pivot point. But that piecemeal approach has made it more difficult to secure the support of a simple majority of Republicans in the House and the Senate. That said, legislative initiatives that can bypass the filibuster offer Trump the greatest opportunity for success. As such, passage of the American Health Care Act as well as tax reform seem the most likely legislative accomplishments for the president, though success on either front has thus far eluded him. Efforts to reform immigration policy, rebuild the nation's aging infrastructure, or build a wall along the border with Mexico are likely to depend on the respective pivot points for each and not simply on the Republican Party's control of Congress.

Table 3.1. Major Legislative Accomplishments during First and Second Year

President	First Year	Second Year
Clinton	Family and Medical Leave Act National Voter Registration Act Omnibus Budget Reconciliation Act National and Community Service Trust Act Religious Freedom Restoration Act Brady Handgun Violence Prevention Act	Freedom of Access to Clinic Entrances Act Violent Crime Control and Law Enforcement Act Violence Against Women Act Improving America's Schools Act Communications Assistance for Law Enforcement Act California Desert Protection Act
Bush[1]	Economic Growth and Tax Relief Reconciliation Act USA PATRIOT Act	No Child Left Behind Act Job Creation and Worker Assistance Act Bipartisan Campaign Reform Act Farm Security and Rural Investment Act Public Company Accounting Reform and Investor Protection Act Joint Resolution to Authorize the Use of United States Armed Forces Against Iraq Homeland Security Act
Obama	American Recovery and Reinvestment Act Credit Card Accountability Responsibility and Disclosure (CARD) Act Lilly Ledbetter Fair Pay Act Children's Health Insurance Program Reauthorization Act Matthew Shepard and James Byrd, Jr. Hate Crimes Prevention Act	Tax Relief, Unemployment Insurance Reauthorization, and Job Creation Act Patient Protection and Affordable Care Act Don't Ask, Don't Tell Repeal Act Budget Control Act Dodd–Frank Wall Street Reform and Consumer Protection Act
Trump		

[1]Bush's narrow Republican majority in the US Senate became a narrow Democratic majority in May 2001 when Vermont senator Jim Jeffords bolted from the Republican Party and declared himself an Independent who would caucus with Senate Democrats. However, the attacks of September 11, 2001, produced a period of bipartisan cooperation and considerable legislative success.

By and With the Advice and Consent of the Senate

The first test of Trump's relationship with Democrats came as his nominees for the cabinet and other executive positions came before the US Senate. Though the relationship between any president and Congress is crucial to the success or failure of a president's legislative agenda, the relationship between a president and the Senate encompasses far more than just legislation. The Senate is responsible for the ratification of treaties negotiated by an administration, and the Senate is responsible for approving most high-level executive branch employees, especially cabinet secretaries. An uncooperative Senate can delay the confirmation of appointees, confirmation hearings can be used as political theater to give voice to opponents of a president's agenda, and in recent years opposition party members in the Senate have used the power of the filibuster to block some nominees. Such difficulties in the Senate can hinder a new president's ability to capitalize on any momentum that may exist following his election. Given the importance of the first two years, as detailed in the prior section, any such delays can have serious repercussions for a president.

In many respects, Trump should have enjoyed unprecedented success with regard to Senate confirmation of his nominees because there is no cloture pivot point. In a highly controversial move in 2013, a Senate Democratic majority ended the filibuster of executive nominees for all positions except for the Supreme Court. As such, Donald Trump was the first newly elected president to enter office with a partisan majority in the Senate and a minority party with no meaningful procedural weapons for derailing a nominee. But the initial willingness of Senate Democrats to vote in favor of many of Trump's nominees caused outrage among the party's liberal base (Nwanevu 2017). By the end of January 2017, activists were demanding greater opposition from Senate Democrats (Bradner 2017). In response to their near powerless state, Democrats in the Senate settled for a strategy of at least delaying nominations that they could not defeat. Such efforts included the boycotting of committee meetings to prevent votes to send nominees to the full Senate for consideration (Pear and Lichtblau 2017). It was an unprecedented strategy. Surprisingly, Trump lags behind his most recent predecessors with regard to both putting forward nominees and getting nominees confirmed within the first 100 days. Bill Clinton had submitted nearly 180 nominees and Barack Obama had submitted just shy of 200 nominees by the 100-day mark. Trump had submitted only 75. Even George W. Bush had submitted nearly 90 nominees within the first 100 days in spite of a compressed transition period resulting from the disputed 2000 election results. Even though Democrats cannot filibuster Trump's nominees, far fewer were confirmed within the first 100 days than for any recent president (O'Connell 2017). Though Trump had submitted a comparable number of cabinet secretaries and undersecretaries, he had submitted but a fraction of the number of assistant secretaries typically put forward during the initial months of a new administration (table 3.2). Specific policy areas and objectives are typically delegated to assistant secretaries and as such they are essential to the effective functioning of the executive branch (O'Connell 2017). As discussed in chapter 4, the executive branch appointees are crucial to the development and promotion of President Trump's agenda.

Table 3.2. Number of Submitted and Confirmed Nominations in the First 100 Days

President	Number of Nominations	Number Confirmed
Clinton	177	49
Bush 43	87	35
Obama	196	70
Trump	75	28

Adapted from Anne Joseph O'Connell, "Trump's Staffing Record in the First 100 Days Was Slow, but Not Catastrophic," *Politico*, May 1, 2017.

Beyond executive branch employees, the Senate has the power to decide who will populate the federal judiciary. Though presidents nominate judges, the Senate must approve them. The politics surrounding judicial confirmations have become especially contentions in recent decades. It is easy to understand the contentious nature of judicial politics once one considers the impact federal courts have on domestic policy. The power of judicial review becomes paramount in an era when gridlock stymies the legislative process and presidents look to claims of broad executive power to bypass the legislative process in the making of policy. Compared to courts in other democracies, the US federal judiciary is more powerful than most, and perhaps the most powerful judiciary in the world. There are several reasons for this, including that the US Constitution is shorter and covers far fewer topics than typical national constitutions. As a result, there is more opportunity for courts to fill in the blanks as new issues arise. Additionally, we tend to view the Constitution as sacred and rarely amend it. This means the courts must answer complex questions about matters of law and policy within the context of rules written more than 200 years ago.

It should be of little surprise that when Supreme Court Justice Antonin Scalia passed away unexpectedly in February 2016, the battle over confirmation of his replacement would be pitched and partisan. Within hours of Scalia's death, Republican Senate Majority Leader Mitch McConnell announced that no hearings or confirmation votes would be held prior to the 2016 presidential election. McConnell said that a successor to Scalia should be determined by the American people and the next president (Everett and Thrush 2016). McConnell's refusal to consider any nominee submitted by President Obama was unprecedented and signaled that partisan politics in the Senate had ascended to new heights. Though White House officials had expected McConnell to block any nominee who was submitted, they had not expected him to shut the door on even considering a nominee. When President Obama submitted Merrick Garland, the well-respected chief judge on the United States Court of Appeals for the District of Columbia, McConnell stayed true to his word and refused consideration.

President Trump nominated Judge Neil Gorsuch of the United States Court of Appeals for the Tenth Circuit on January 31, 2017, to succeed Scalia. Like Garland, Gorsuch was a widely respected jurist who had received clear bipartisan support in the Senate for his prior confirmation. Though many Senate Democrats expressed a willingness to give Gorsuch their full consideration, many party activists (and Senate Democrats) were angry over the treatment of the Garland nomination. Under the leadership of Minority Leader Chuck Schumer (D-NY), Democrats pondered how to proceed with the Gorsuch confirmation. As the minority party, Democrats lacked the power to block outright consideration of Gorsuch. So they could not replicate the GOP strategy used against Garland. Additionally, some questioned whether there was sufficient cause to mount an all-out opposition to Gorsuch given that he was a conservative judge being nominated to replace a conservative justice. As such, his appointment would not alter the ideological balance of the Supreme Court. Perhaps Senate Democrats would be better served to hold their fire and instead wage a battle against a future nominee whose appointment would affect the balance of the court (Foran 2017). Additionally, surveys showed that Democratic voters were less motivated than Republicans over the makeup of the Supreme Court, and several Senate Democrats up for reelection 2018 were from states won by Donald Trump. Democrats understood as well that should they attempt to block Gorsuch's nomination via filibuster, the Republican majority was likely to eliminate the filibuster of Supreme Court nominees—an extension of the filibuster change pushed through by Democrats in 2013. Such a move would leave Democrats powerless to block a future nominee who may well tip the balance of the court (Foran 2017).

As the Gorsuch confirmation hearings began in March 2017 Democrats were still without a settled strategy, and it appeared that Gorsuch was heading for confirmation. Though many Democrats had announced their opposition to Gorsuch, the party lacked the 41 votes necessary to sustain a filibuster. Over several days of contentious hearings, Democratic committee members grilled Gorsuch over his opinions in cases involving the rights of employees, students with intellectual disabilities, and his actions in support of executive power while in the Justice Department under the George W. Bush administration (Flegenheimer et al. 2017). On the final day of hearings, Minority Leader Schumer announced that he would oppose the Gorsuch nomination and urged Senate Democrats to join him in the effort to block Gorsuch (Barnes, O'Keefe, and Marimow 2017). In response, the Republican leadership announced that Gorsuch would be confirmed, even if it meant changing the filibuster rules.

A small group of Republican and Democratic senators worked behind the scenes in an effort to craft a compromise to avert the threatened filibuster and rules changes even as Democratic leadership worked to secure the 41 votes needed to sustain the filibuster (Mascaro 2017). Shortly after the Senate Judiciary Committee voted, along party lines, to send the Gorsuch nomination to the full Senate, it was announced that Democrats had secured 42 votes in support of the filibuster. No compromise would be reached (Mascaro 2017). The confirmation vote took place on April 7, 2017. When Democrats blocked the effort to proceed to a vote, Majority Leader Mitch McConnell invoked what has been called "the nuclear option" of changing Senate rules with a simple majority vote. All 52 Republicans voted to eliminate the filibuster of Supreme Court nominees (Shabad 2017). Gorsuch was ultimately confirmed by a vote of 54–45, with only 3 Democrats (each up for election in 2018 from states carried by Donald Trump) voting along with all Republicans (Cameron et al. 2017).

The Gorsuch confirmation was not the first time the Senate had been brought to the brink of ending all judicial filibusters. In 2005 Republican Senate leadership, frustrated with Democratic filibusters of President Bush's judicial nominees, decided "go nuclear" and end the filibuster. A bipartisan group of seven Republicans and seven Democrats, known as the

Gang of 14, negotiated a compromise. Under their agreement, Democrats would reserve the filibuster for use under extraordinary circumstance, and Republicans would preserve the filibuster. The Gang of 14 included enough Democrats to prevent the party from mounting a successful filibuster and enough Republicans to prevent the party from going nuclear (CNN 2005).

In the week preceding the vote to confirm Gorsuch a bipartisan group of nine senators, four Democrats and five Republicans, met to discuss a compromise that would preserve the filibuster and confirm Gorsuch. The failure of that effort highlights important changes that have taken place in the Senate—changes that will affect President Trump's legislative agenda. Democratic senator Chris Coons summed up the cause of the failure quite well: "[Republicans] had a hard time trusting that we wouldn't just filibuster the next nominee. . . . We had a hard time trusting that they wouldn't just break the rules on the next nominee" (Everett and Kim 2017). The Gang of 14 compromise succeeded in 2005 because the members trusted each other and had faith that each would keep his word. Such trust was largely gone by 2017—especially regarding the filibuster. The years between 2005 and 2017 witnessed deep hypocrisy over the issue on both sides of the aisle. Republicans, who had decried the use of the filibuster when they were in the majority, used it extensively against President Obama once they found themselves in the minority. And Democrats, who had declared the filibuster essential to the concept of checks and balance while in the minority, stripped it away once they were in the majority.

THE CONGRESSIONAL REVIEW ACT

Trump's difficulties achieving his proactive policy agenda in Congress cannot overshadow the early and significant successes in his reactive efforts to dismantle President Obama's regulatory legacy. Working with Congress, the Trump White House made use of a rather obscure piece of federal law, the Congressional Review Act. On April 25, 2017, the Trump White House marked the hundredth day of the new administration with a press release heralding the president's legislative record. According to the release, President Trump had signed "more legislation in his first 100 days than any President since Truman" (White House 2017). What followed was a list of recent presidents and the total pieces of legislation signed by each during their first 100 days. Indeed, at 28 laws, Trump had signed more legislation than any presidents since Truman's 55 laws. To better understand President Trump's touted legislative accomplishments, it is necessary to understand just what the Congressional Review Act (CRA) is, given that nearly half of the legislation signed by President Trump during his first 100 days were CRA resolutions.

The CRA was attached to the Small Business Regulatory Enforcement Fairness Act signed by President Clinton in 1996. The CRA represented an ongoing effort on the part of congressional Republicans to reclaim some degree of power over the executive branch and the administrative state. Stated plainly, the CRA empowers Congress to enact a "resolution of disapproval," which, if signed by the president or by veto-override, would overturn a regulation issued by an executive branch agency. Once overturned, the issuing agency would be barred from reintroducing the rejected regulation or any substantively similar regulation unless authorized by congressional action. Unlike most pieces of legislation, a CRA resolution cannot be filibustered in the Senate. In effect, the law gives newly elected presidents and Congresses, when acting together, an effective and streamlined approach to overturn regulations issued during the waning months and weeks of outgoing administrations ("Mysteries" 2009). But the power is not unlimited. A resolution of disapproval under the CRA must be passed within 60 legislative days (days when Congress is in session) of being issued. Because of the 60-day clock, the CRA is viewed as a tool likely only to be used during presidential transitions and under unified government.

Knowing that time was limited, lawmakers and members of Trump's staff held weekly meetings to prepare a list of regulations, enacted during the final six months of Obama's presidency, that would be good targets for CRA disapproval (Shear 2017). In the end, Trump and the Republican Congress successfully rejected 14 regulations issued by President Obama during his final months in office (table 3.3). Trump's use of the CRA and the number of resolutions signed by him were unprecedented. In the 20 years following its creation, the CRA had been used successfully a single time by President George W. Bush during his first month in office—one time in 20 years. Trump used it to overturn 14 regulations in the span of four months. Among the regulations overturned by Congress were new rules requiring coal companies to ensure that mountaintop mining runoff was not polluting local waterways; requiring the Social Security Administration to provide information about mentally incapacitated people to law enforcement agencies conducting background checks for gun purchases;

preventing Internet service providers from collecting, sharing, or selling a customer's information without permission; and preventing states from denying funding for women's health services to facilities that also provided abortions. Because the CRA prohibits a federal agency from reissuing substantive similar regulations once a CRA resolution has been approved, Trump's successful use of the CRA is likely to have an impact on regulations well into the future.

Table 3.3. Congressional Review Act under President Trump

Date	Title	Description
February 14, 2017	H.J.Res. 41	Providing for congressional disapproval of a rule submitted by the Securities and Exchange Commission relating to "Disclosure of Payments by Resource Extraction Issuers"
February 16, 2017	H.J.Res. 38	Disapproving the rule submitted by the Department of the Interior known as the "Stream Protection Rule"
February 28, 2017	H.J.Res. 40	Providing for congressional disapproval of the rule submitted by the Social Security Administration relating to implementation of the NICS Improvement Amendments Act of 2007
March 27, 2017	H.J.Res. 37	Disapproving the rule submitted by the Department of Defense, the General Services Administration, and the National Aeronautics and Space Administration relating to the Federal Acquisition Regulation
March 27, 2017	H.J.Res. 44	Disapproving the rule submitted by the Department of the Interior relating to Bureau of Land Management regulations that establish the procedures used to prepare, revise, or amend land use plans pursuant to the Federal Land Policy and Management Act of 1976
March 27, 2017	H.J.Res. 57	Providing for congressional disapproval of the rule submitted by the Department of Education relating to accountability and state plans under the Elementary and Secondary Education Act of 1965
March 27, 2017	H.J.Res. 58	Providing for congressional disapproval of the rule submitted by the Department of Education relating to teacher preparation issues
March 31, 2017	H.J.Res. 42	Disapproving the rule submitted by the Department of Labor relating to drug testing of unemployment compensation applicants
April 3, 2017	H.J.Res. 69	Providing for congressional disapproval of the final rule of the Department of the Interior relating to "Non-Subsistence Take of Wildlife, and Public Participation and Closure Procedures, on National Wildlife Refuges in Alaska"

Table 3.3. Congressional Review Act under President Trump (*continued*)

Date	Title	Description
April 3, 2017	H.J.Res. 83	Disapproving the rule submitted by the Department of Labor relating to "Clarification of Employer's Continuing Obligation to Make and Maintain an Accurate Record of Each Recordable Injury and Illness"
April 3, 2017	S.J.Res. 34	Providing for congressional disapproval of the rule submitted by the Federal Communications Commission relating to "Protecting the Privacy of Customers of Broadband and Other Telecommunications Services"
April 13, 2017	H.J.Res. 43	Providing for congressional disapproval of the final rule submitted by Secretary of Health and Human Services relating to compliance with Title X requirements by project recipients in selecting subrecipients
April 13, 2017	H.J.Res. 67	Disapproving the rule submitted by the Department of Labor relating to savings arrangements established by qualified state political subdivisions for nongovernmental employees
May 17, 2017	H.J.Res. 66	Disapproving the rule submitted by the Department of Labor relating to savings arrangements established by states for nongovernmental employees

INITIAL ASSESSMENT OF TRUMP'S EARLY RECORD WITH CONGRESS

As a candidate, Trump touted his ability to make deals and suggested that he could achieve immediate successes in Congress. Indeed, he proposed an ambitious 100-day agenda that included a dozen pieces of significant legislation. But as Trump's first 100 days slowly crept toward his first 365 days he had not moved that legislative agenda forward, contradicting the image he had presented as skilled deal maker. Though Trump blamed Democratic obstructionism, many frustrated Republicans in Congress viewed Trump as the source of the problem (Caldwell 2017a). As detailed in chapter 2, the ongoing House and Senate investigations into Russian influence over the 2016 elections were consuming considerable time and resources. Trump's decision to fire FBI director James Comey only served to intensify the pressure to investigate the matter and added the specter of possible obstruction of justice charges against Trump (Bennett 2017).

Even without the distraction of the Russia investigation, Trump has created obstacles for his agenda. In mid-June 2017 it was reported that Senate Republicans were nearing a deal on legislation to repeal and replace the Affordable Care Act. Republican leadership was struggling to secure the 50 votes needed, and conservative senators were the main obstacle. Leadership could afford no more than 2 Republican defections, assuming no Democrats support the GOP legislation. Senators Rand Paul (R-KY) and Mike Lee (R-UT) opposed the legislation, as they felt that it did not go far enough. Senator Ted Cruz, who had long agreed with Paul and Lee, was willing to work with leadership to construct legislation that he could support (Sullivan and Snell 2017). As those negotiations were taking place, President Trump held a meeting with Senate Republicans and said that the House-passed version of the legislation, which he once referred to as "great" and "well crafted," was mean, and he wanted the Senate to craft a bill that was more generous and added more money. Such changes likely would make it more difficult to secure the support of conservatives in the Senate or in the House.

As the Senate negotiations entered a critical phase in early July 2017, Trump disrupted the process by suggesting that the Congress instead simply vote to repeal the ACA and worry later about replacing it. By the end of July the Senate's repeal and replace bill was dead, as four Republican senators refused to support it. What followed was a dizzying display of efforts to cobble together something to help Republicans save face. President Trump did little to settle matters. In a span of 36 hours, following the demise of the repeal and replace bill, Trump took three contradictory positions. First, he urged the Senate to simply repeal the ACA and work on a replacement later. Less than ten hours later he said that he believed that the ACA should be left alone to fail so that a better plan could be developed in the aftermath. Finally, Trump took to Twitter just 24 hours later and urged Republicans to do a better job selling their repeal and replace bill to the public (Rupar 2017). By August, it seemed clear that repeal and replace was dead.

Trump's frustration over the failure of the repeal and replace was evident, and he directed much of his anger toward Senate Majority Leader Mitch McConnell. Trump suggested that McConnell was responsible for the failure and questioned whether he was an effective leader. Those close to McConnell indicated that the majority leader was blindsided by the attacks. Others questioned the logic behind the attack. Sara Fagen, a former senior aide to President George W. Bush, described the attack on McConnell as the "single dumbest thing Donald Trump's done in office" (Fox 2017). Though Fagen's comment may be a bit hyperbolic, Trump's legislative agenda has languished during his first year in office. As majority leader, and a master of Senate rules and procedures, McConnell is a crucial ally for the president. Trump needs McConnell on his side. Though McConnell is not very popular among Trump's political base, poisoning that relationship makes little strategic sense.

The House and Senate demonstrated as well that they are not beholden to Trump's agenda. In late July 2017 the House and Senate bucked the wishes of the White House by approving new sanctions against Russia. By a vote of 419–3 in the House and 98–2 in the Senate, the bill to target Russia's aggression in Ukraine and Syria was sent to Trump. Though Trump threatened to veto the measure, there were more than sufficient votes to override the veto. Although Vice President Pence has fulfilled his expected role as a liaison between the White House and Congress, there's little to suggest that his close relationship with congressional Republicans has delivered much in the way of legislative victories. Pence played a key role behind the scenes in the Senate as the chamber considered the repeal and replace of the Affordable Care Act and personally lobbied John McCain just moments before the senator cast the vote to deny President Trump one of his biggest campaign promises. Perhaps Pence's greatest accomplishment in the early days of Trump's relationship with Congress is his ability to soothe and assuage the concerns of congressional Republicans when Trump missteps or distracts from the party's legislative agenda.

The clear lack of cross-party confidence and trust evident in the Gorsuch confirmation battle suggests that Trump's legislative agenda will rise and fall along with Republican fortunes in the Senate. He may not be able to count on winning over much, if any, Democratic support. President Trump acknowledged that reality in late May 2017 when he took to Twitter and urged the Senate to "switch to 51 votes, immediately" for passing legislation. Trump endorsed the outright end of the filibuster. Indeed, many analysts see that as the inevitable outcome of the 2013 and 2017 changes to the filibuster for nominees (Chafetz 2017a). Trump's struggles with the repeal of the Affordable Care Act make clear that the Republican Party's 2-seat Senate majority provides little breathing room for dissent. Even with Vice President Pence's tie-breaking vote, Trump can lose no more than 2 Republican senators on any issue unless he can win over at least some Democrats.

So far, Trump's greatest legislative successes have been the negation of Obama-era regulations via the Congressional Review Act. Such successes ought not be dismissed. But Trump promised an aggressive legislative and policy agenda that extended well beyond rolling back a handful of last-minute regulations issued by the Obama administration. In order to keep the promises made during the campaign, Trump needs Congress. He needs true legislative successes if he is to repeal and replace the Affordable Care Act or reform the tax code. He needs a disciplined and focused message regarding his legislative agenda. His ever-escalating Twitter battles with the press have not helped. The clock is running on the window of opportunity afforded most presidents during their first two years in office. But Trump faces the challenges of a slender Republican majority in the Senate, unified Democratic opposition, and limited political capital.

WORKS CITED

Abramson, Alana. "Health Care Bill: Donald Trump Says It's 'Ok' If It Fails." *Time*. July 2, 2017.

Barnes, Robert, Ed O'Keefe, and Ann E. Marimow. "Schumer: Democrats Will Filibuster Gorsuch Nomination." *Washington Post*. March 23, 2017.

Beckwith, Ryan Teague, Philip Elliott, and Alana Abramson. "Health Care Senate Vote Delayed Until after July 4." *Time*. July 2, 2017.

Bennett, John T. "Legislative Agenda Gets Tougher for Trump." *Roll Call*. June 12, 2017.

Bierman, Noah. "Trump Opens 'Infrastructure Week' without a Plan, and Calls for Privatizing Air Traffic Control." *Los Angeles Times*. July 4, 2017.

Bradner, Eric. "Democrats Feeling Heat to Oppose Trump's Picks." CNN. January 30, 2017.

Bryan, Bob. "Senate Republicans Signal They Plan to Scrap Bill the House Just Passed and Write Their Own." *Business Insider*. May 4, 2017.

Caldwell, Leigh Ann. "Lawmakers Declare President Trump's Budget Proposal 'Dead on Arrival.'" NBCNews.com. May 23, 2017a.

Caldwell, Leigh Ann. "Trump Drama Imperils GOP Legislative Agenda." NBCNews.com. May 21, 2017b.

Cameron, Darla, Kevin Schaul, Kim Soffen, and Kevin Uhrmacher. "How the Senate Voted to Alter Its Rules on Supreme Court Appointments." *Washington Post*. June 14, 2017.

Chafetz, Josh. "Perspective | The Filibuster Was Already Doomed before the Nuclear Option Vote." *Washington Post*. April 6, 2017a.

Chafetz, Josh. "The Real 'Resistance' to Trump? The GOP Congress." *Politico*. June 6, 2017b.

CNN. "Senators Compromise on Filibusters." June 15, 2005.

Collier, Kenneth E. *Between the Branches: The White House Office of Legislative Affairs*. Pittsburgh, PA: University of Pittsburgh, 1997.

Everett, Burgess, and Josh Dawsey. "Trump to Warring GOP Senators: I'm On Your Side." *Politico*. June 28, 2017. Accessed July 8, 2017. http://www.politico.com/story/2017/06/28/trump-health-care-paul-collins-240065.

Everett, Burgess, and Seung Min Kim. "Inside the Failed Secret Mission to Save the Filibuster." *Politico*. April 8, 2017. Accessed August 22, 2017. http://www.politico.com/story/2017/04/neil-gorsuch-filibuster-negotiations-237009.

Everett, Burgess, Louis Nelson, and Adam Cancryn. "Trump Further Disrupts Obamacare Repeal Efforts." *Politico*. June 30, 2017. Accessed August 22, 2017. http://www.politico.com/story/2017/06/30/trump-obamacare-repeal-replace-tweet-240132.

Everett, Burgess, and Glenn Thrush. "McConnell Throws Down the Gauntlet: No Scalia Replacement under Obama." *Politico*. February 13, 2016. Accessed August 22, 2017. http://www.politico.com/story/2016/02/mitch-mcconnell-antonin-scalia-supreme-court-nomination-219248.

Flegenheimer, Matt, Carl Hulse, Charlie Savage, and Adam Liptak. "Six Highlights From the Gorsuch Confirmation Hearing." *New York Times*. March 20, 2017.

Foran, Clare. "Why Are Democrats Holding Back on Gorsuch?" *The Atlantic*. March 20, 2017.

Fox, Michelle. "Former Bush Aide: This Is the 'Single Dumbest Thing' Trump Has Done in Office." CNBC. August 14, 2017.

Gallup, Inc. "Presidential Approval Ratings—Gallup Historical Statistics and Trends." Gallup.com. June 5, 2017.

Hellmann, Jessie. "GOP Senator: Healthcare Deal Unlikely This Year." *The Hill*. June 2, 2017.

Hohmann, James. "Analysis | The Daily 202: Trump Dysfunction Follows Family from the Campaign to the White House." *Washington Post*. July 12, 2017a.

Hohmann, James. "Analysis | The Daily 202: Trump's Hardball Tactics Backfire as 'Skinny Repeal' Goes Down." *Washington Post*. July 28, 2017b.

Huetteman, Emmarie, and Nicholas Kulish. "House Passes 2 Strict Immigration Bills, at Trump's Urging." *New York Times*. June 29, 2017.

Kaplan, Thomas, and Robert Pear. "Health Bill Would Add 24 Million Uninsured but Save $337 Billion, Report Says." *New York Times*. March 13, 2017a.

Kaplan, Thomas, and Robert Pear. "Senate Health Bill Would Leave 22 Million More Uninsured, C.B.O. Says." *New York Times*. June 26, 2017b.

Kaplan, Thomas, Jennifer Steinhauer, and Robert Pear. "Trump, in Zigzag, Calls House Republicans' Health Bill 'Mean.'" *New York Times*. June 13, 2017.

Kelly, Amita, and Barbara Sprunt. "Here Is What Donald Trump Wants to Do in His First 100 Days." NPR. November 9, 2016.

Lee, M. J., Lauren Fox, and Phil Mattingly. "Senate Finally Unveils Secret Health Care Bill." CNN. June 22, 2017.

Los Angeles Times. "'I Will Be President for All Americans'—Transcript of Donald Trump's Election Night Victory Speech." November 9, 2016.

Mascaro, Lisa. "Senators Work Quietly on Long-Shot Bid for Compromise as Democrats Secure Votes to Filibuster Gorsuch." *Los Angeles Times.* June 14, 2017.

Mayhew, David R. *Divided We Govern: Party Control, Lawmaking and Investigations, 1946–2002.* New Haven, CT: Yale University Press, 2005.

Merica, Dan, Lauren Fox, and M. J. Lee. "Senate to White House on Health Care: No Trump, Please." CNN. June 22, 2017.

"The Mysteries of the Congressional Review Act." *Harvard Law Review* (122). June 1, 2009. Accessed August 22, 2017. https://harvardlawreview.org/2009/06/the-mysteries-of-the-congressional-review-act/.

Neustadt, Richard E. *Presidential Power and the Modern Presidents: The Politics of Leadership from Roosevelt to Reagan.* New York: Free Press, 1991.

Nwanevu, Osita. "Here Are the Senate Democrats Who Have Voted for Trump's Nominees." *Slate.* January 27, 2017.

O'Brien, Matt. "Perspective | Trump Keeps Pretending His Infrastructure Plan Is Real. It's Not." *Washington Post.* June 8, 2017.

O'Connell, Anne Joseph. "Trump's Staffing Record in the First 100 Days Was Slow, but Not Catastrophic." Brookings Institution. May 5, 2017.

Pear, Robert, and Eric Lichtblau. "Senate Democrats Delay Confirmation of Mnuchin and Price." *New York Times.* January 31, 2017.

Pearlstein, Steven. "Perspective | Mark This Date: Donald Trump Is Now a Lame-Duck President." *Washington Post.* July 28, 2017.

Pfiffner, James P., and Roger H. Davidson. *Understanding the Presidency.* Boston: Pearson, 2013.

Politifact, and Robert Pittenger, US Representative. "Does the AHCA Protect Pre-existing Conditions?" *@politifact.* May 5, 2017.

Rupar, Aaron. "Trump Has Changed His Health Care Stance 3 Times in Past 36 Hours. Here Are the Receipts." ThinkProgress. July 19, 2017.

Savransky, Rebecca. "GOP Senator under Impression Trump Doesn't Have Clear Understanding of Healthcare Bill: Report." *The Hill.* June 28, 2017.

Schreckinger, Ben, Annie Karni, Nick Gass, Jack Shafer, Ben Wofford, and Joel S. Baden. "Trump Attacks McCain: 'I Like People Who Weren't Captured.'" *Politico.* July 19, 2015.

Shabad, Rebecca. "Senate 'Nuclear Option' Invoked in Gorsuch Confirmation Vote." CBS News. April 6, 2017.

Shear, Michael D. "Trump Discards Obama Legacy, One Rule at a Time." *New York Times*. May 1, 2017.

Silver, Nate. "War Is Peace. Freedom Is Slavery. Trump Won in a Landslide." FiveThirtyEight. November 28, 2016.

Sullivan, Sean, and Kelsey Snell. "Cruz's Fragile Alliance with GOP Leaders Now Pivotal in Health-Care Push." *Washington Post*. June 13, 2017.

Taylor, Andrew. "GOP-Controlled House Subcommittees Reject Trump Budget Cuts." *Washington Post*. June 28, 2017.

Thurber, James A., and Jordan Tama. *Rivals for Power: Presidential-Congressional Relations*. Lanham, MD: Rowman & Littlefield, 2017.

Wagner, John. "Trump Touts 'Amazing' Progress, Basks in Praise of His Cabinet." *Washington Post*. June 12, 2017.

White House, United States Government. "President Trump's 100 Days of Historic Accomplishments." April 25, 2017.

4

Trump and Domestic Policy

@realDonaldTrump
If elected, I will undo all of Obama's executive orders. I will deliver.
Let's Make America Great Again!
(2:09:54 p.m., May 4, 2015)

@realDonaldTrump
Great numbers on the economy. All of our work, including the passage
of many bills & regulation killing Executive Orders, now kicking in!
(9:14:29 p.m., June 11, 2017)

As a US senator, Barack Obama was highly critical of President George
W. Bush's use of unilateral executive action to make policy without
Congress. Obama viewed this exercise of unilateral power as troubling. As
a presidential candidate in 2008, Obama pledged to review every executive
action issued by Bush and to have his attorney general determine which
actions were legal and which were not. Obama followed through on his
pledge and reversed many of Bush's executive actions within months of
assuming the presidency. President Obama had a change of heart regarding the propriety of unilateral executive action after Republicans retook
the House of Representatives in 2010. Donald Trump was equally critical
of President Obama's use of executive power and pledged to undo every
executive action Obama had issued. In many respects, simply undoing

many of Obama's executive actions is a significant component of President Trump's domestic policy agenda. All of this raises some important questions: Can an incoming president simply wipe the slate clean of his predecessor's executive actions? How many types of executive actions exist and how do they differ? Would the undoing of Obama's executive actions truly be a substantive accomplishment for President Trump?

Donald Trump made many bold promises as a candidate. His promises can be categorized into those he can deliver under his authority as chief executive and those that will require the support of Congress. His policy agenda can be further categorized into reactive and proactive proposals. Actions taken to reverse or undo Obama-era policies are mostly reactive, while proposals for new or revised programs are proactive. Tax reform and building a border wall are proactive measures that require Congress. Rolling back Obama-era executive actions is mostly unilateral and reactive. But the repeal and replace of the Affordable Care Act is more difficult to categorize. Given that the Affordable Care Act may be more likely to be replaced or reformed and not repealed, it may be best viewed as a proactive proposal rather than reactive, although executive actions taken by Trump to lessen the impact of the Affordable Care Act would be reactive. Likewise, the undoing of some established Obama-era regulations, a reactive approach, will require Congress. The following pages should add clarity to the categorizations as well as the challenges to each.

Throughout this chapter special emphasis is placed on those things that Trump can accomplish without Congress. Promises to modernize the nation's infrastructure, to build a wall along the US-Mexico border, to repeal and replace the Affordable Care Act, or to overhaul the tax code will require legislation and therefore support from congressional Republicans and (in many cases) from enough Senate Democrats to overcome likely filibuster attempts. Many House and Senate Republicans openly opposed Trump's candidacy, and only time will tell if they are willing to fall in line as members of the same party. As detailed in chapter 3, Trump has not replicated the first-year legislative record of Bill Clinton or Barack Obama in the area of proactive policy success. His struggles with Congress are discussed in that chapter, and sources of his troubles in general are discussed at the end of this chapter. Trump did, however, enjoy considerable reactive policy accomplishments early in his first year, both unilaterally and in Congress, as he set about dismantling significant parts Obama's policy legacy.

TRUMP'S DOMESTIC AGENDA

Prior to discussing President Trump's record on domestic policy it is useful to revisit the domestic agenda put forward by candidate Trump. Though Trump's domestic agenda often lacked specificity, there are policies or policy areas that he discussed since the day he announced his candidacy in June 2015. In his announcement speech, Trump pledged to build a wall along the border with Mexico and to deport people in the United States illegally, he pledged to rejuvenate domestic manufacturing by renegotiating or abandoning trade deals, he promised to repeal and replace the Affordable Care Act, to protect the Second Amendment, to rebuild America's infrastructure, and to protect Social Security, Medicare, and Medicaid. And, quite significantly, he promised to reduce what he described as "massive job-killing" regulations (Kopan 2016). Trump focused much of his ire on environmental regulations that he believed to be undermining the US energy sector, especially with regard to extracting fossil fuels such as oil, natural gas, and coal.

Much of this chapter explores Trump's pledge to roll back regulations, because this approach may yield greater success for Trump than for most of his predecessors. Much of President Obama's domestic policy legacy, from immigration to environmental policy, was constructed using unilateral executive action and new or revised regulations issued by federal agencies under his lead (Schier and Eberly 2013; Crews 2016). President Trump is likely to use his power as chief executive to roll back many of those actions. In fact, as a candidate Trump promised to repeal "every single Obama executive order" (Kopan 2016). Never before has an incoming president had an agenda so focused on undoing the agenda of the outgoing president.

Trump's approach to rolling back Obama-era executive actions and regulations is directed by the type of action being targeted. Executive actions come in several different flavors. Excluding regulations and international executive agreements (which will be discussed separately), there are three main types of executive actions—executive orders, presidential memoranda, and presidential proclamations. Each has a different level of authority and impact, but historically executive orders carry the most authority and tend to be subject to most public scrutiny. By law, executive orders must be numbered sequentially, must contain a clear statement of the president's legal authority to issue the order, and must be published in the *Federal Register* (official government publication used to announce changes to government requirements, policies, and guidance to the public). They are similar in effect to laws passed by Congress and typically direct members of the executive branch to follow a new policy or directive. Though the number of executive orders issued by presidents has declined in recent decades, the scope and scale of the orders issued has increased dramatically (Nelson 2010). Trump issued 32 executive orders during his first 100 days in office—more than any president since Truman (Cohen and Payson-Denney 2017). President Obama issued 19 in his first 100 days compared to 11 by George W. Bush and 13 by Bill Clinton.

Presidential memoranda are not required to be either published or numbered, and they are typically used to delegate responsibilities already assigned to the executive branch by Congress. It's important to note that the line between an executive order and a presidential memorandum has blurred in recent years. President Obama made considerable use of memoranda for purposes once considered more appropriate to executive orders. For example, President Obama created the Deferred Action for Childhood Arrivals (DACA) program via presidential memorandum in 2013. DACA allows certain undocumented persons, who entered the country as minors, to receive a renewable two-year period of deferred action from deportation as well as eligibility for a work permit. The provisions set forth in the DACA policy were very similar to a legislative proposal that was defeated in Congress in 2010. President Obama was able to resurrect much of the proposed law by using his executive authority to direct the heads of US Customs and Border Protection (CBP), US Citizenship and Immigration Services (USCIS), and US Immigration and Customs Enforcement (ICE) to "de-prioritize" the enforcement of immigration laws with regard to the individuals who met the requirements established in the directive. As this example makes clear, memoranda are often just executive orders by another name (Cooper 2014). Memoranda are attractive to presidents because they are less public. They are not numbered, there are no requirements for publication, and they can have the same effect as executive orders. President Obama, a one-time critic of unilateral executive actions, refuted criticism of his executive actions by claiming that he issued fewer executive orders than most of his predecessors. Technically this is true but also very misleading. Obama had issued fewer executive orders, but he made unprecedented use of memoranda during his two terms, issuing more than any prior president (Kessler 2014). And in many cases his memoranda established substantive policies. Trump issued 28 memoranda in his first 100 days as compared to 22 by President Obama.

Presidential proclamations are statements issued by a president on a matter of public policy, but they tend to be ceremonial and do not have the force of law unless authorized by Congress. They are often ceremonial or symbolic in nature. President Trump issued 24 proclamations during his first 100 days, the same number as President Obama. Indicative of their ceremonial nature, President Trump issued a proclamation declaring National Agriculture Day, and President Obama issued a proclamation declaring Read Across America Day.

Moving beyond orders, memoranda, and proclamations we find executive agreements and federal regulations. Executive agreements are made solely by the president with the head of state of one or more foreign governments. Executive agreements may be legally binding if they were entered into pursuant to a president's constitutional powers or as the result of congressional action. Executive agreements entered into by action of the executive branch alone are known as "simple executive agreements." Under customary practice, an agreement that affects domestic law or budget appropriations is submitted for congressional approval via joint resolution. It is generally accepted that executive agreements, especially simple executive agreements, are not binding on future presidents. As a result, a president may terminate the executive agreements entered into by a predecessor.

Federal regulations are issued by federal agencies and commissions to determine how laws are to be implemented and administered. Laws passed by Congress are often vague, and responsibility for specifics falls upon the agency or agencies responsible for enforcing the law. Because the agencies responsible for issuing regulations are organized under the executive branch, rule making affords a president the opportunity to significantly influence and direct policy. This influence is further enhanced because presidents appoint the heads of federal agencies, and appointees are typically supporters of the president's agenda and governing philosophy. But presidents do not have free rein. Federal agencies and presidential appointees are answerable as well to Congress, and all regulations must comply with the Administrative Procedures Act (APA) of 1946. The APA requires that proposed regulations be justified under the law and appropriate to implementing the law. The agency or agencies issuing the regulations must provide an opportunity for public notice and comment when proposing rules and regulations. In most cases, an agency must first issue a notice of proposed rule making and allow a 30-day comment period before issuing a final rule. Once finalized, the rule or regulation has the full force of law.

A president may halt, review, or revise rules and regulations that have yet to be finalized, and most incoming presidents, Trump included, order an immediate halt to and review of all pending regulations issued under his predecessor. Final rules, however, cannot be easily altered without new legislation from Congress. If a president does wish to revise or reverse a final rule, then the agency must go through the entire rule-making process established by the APA—including a justification for the change. The process of reversing or revising a final rule is time and resource intensive, and revisions can be challenged in the federal courts. Revised rules may be rejected by the courts if it's found that they made use of selective information to justify the revision, if the justification for revision runs counter to evidence, or if the revised rule failed to reflect diverse perspectives or expected expertise. Thus efforts made to undo a predecessor's regulatory legacy may come at the expense of establishing a new president's legacy, and there is no guarantee of success (Thurber and Tama 2017). Over his 8 years in the White House, President Obama established an extensive library of final rules. President Trump has targeted some, but his options for revising them may be limited.

TRUMP'S DOMESTIC RECORD

To properly assess Trump's initial efforts it is crucial to understand that no small part of Trump's domestic agenda was premised upon an almost unprecedented commitment to rolling back his predecessor's policy legacy. As previously noted, some of that will require the cooperation of Congress and a successful record of legislative accomplishments. This is especially true when considering Trump's pledge to repeal and replace the Affordable Care Act. We review his progress with that in chapter 3. Other proactive domestic policy promises such as the building of a border wall and modernization of America's aging infrastructure will require as well the cooperation of Congress. But promises to roll back regulations on American industry, to boost domestic energy production, and to undo Obama's environmental policy legacy can, at least in part, be accomplished via the exercise of unilateral executive authority. That is not to imply that the job will be easily or quickly accomplished.

One of the main reasons that Trump can use executive actions to target Obama's domestic policies is that Obama made widespread use of executive action to implement his agenda. Though Obama enjoyed significant legislative success during his first two years in office, that track record ended after Republicans regained control of the House in the 2010 midterm elections. On issues as varied as climate, immigration, and the availability of prescription drugs, Obama was fond of saying (and even tweeting), "If Congress won't act, I will" (Associated Press 2011; Lehmann and Massey 2013). The Obama administration even established a "We Can't Wait" page on the White House website to highlight Obama's unilateral actions. The archive of that page offers a virtual one-stop shop of initiatives for the Trump administration to reverse (Pfeiffer 2017).

On his first day in office, President Trump ordered a halt to all pending regulations to allow for review or revision (Kopan 2017). Such a move is standard practice for incoming presidents. Trump issued as well a seemingly symbolic executive order intended to "minimize the economic burden of the Affordable Care Act." Though much of the order set the stage for future legislative action, one section directed federal agency heads to "waive, defer, grant exemptions or delay implementation of any requirements of the act that would place fiscal burdens" as a result of the Affordable Care Act ("Executive Order" 2017). In response, the Internal Revenue Service announced that they would not implement a process for rejecting tax returns from filers who failed to indicate whether they had insurance coverage. Why does this matter? Much of the Affordable Care Act can be boiled down to two key and interconnected components—insurance companies cannot deny coverage or charge higher premiums due to a preexisting medical condition, and all individuals must purchase health insurance. Insurers are reluctant to offer insurance to individuals with preexisting conditions, as they tend to use more services and incur higher costs. Insurers compensate for those costs by charging more or by refusing to cover expenses related to the preexisting condition. The problem is made worse by the tendency of younger and healthier individuals to forgo the purchase of insurance because they believe that the cost of coverage outweighs the benefits provided. But insurers need the premiums paid by younger and healthier individuals to offset the costs of providing benefits to sicker individuals. To alleviate this concern and encourage participation by private insurers, the Affordable Care Act mandated that all individuals purchase insurance or face a penalty. That penalty was imposed as a tax by the Internal Revenue Service, and the mechanism for enforcing the penalty was individual tax returns.

If the IRS accepts tax returns regardless of whether the filer has answered the question regarding insurance coverage, then neither the mandate nor the penalty would have the intended effect of compelling young and healthy individuals to purchase insurance (Pender 2017). Since the implementation of the Affordable Care Act, enrollments by younger and healthier individuals have consistently underperformed estimates when the law was drafted. As a result, many participating insurers have faced financial losses, prompting premium increases, and many insurers have withdrawn from the program, creating situations throughout the country where consumers lacked a choice of health plans (Goldstein 2017). These developments threatened the sustainability of the program regardless of whether Trump had won the election. The decision by the IRS to not enforce the mandate is likely to exacerbate those exits and further destabilize the program.

In many respects, Trump's order to agency heads to find ways to minimize and defer the potential burdens of the Affordable Care Act is little different from Obama's memo to prioritize immigration enforcement under the DACA program. In both cases, presidents were directing executive branch agencies to use their discretion when enforcing aspects of law. Much as the memorandum establishing the DACA program was challenged in court, Trump's order is likewise susceptible to judicial challenge. Unless Congress intervenes, the order will remain in effect until a court renders a decision or the order is rescinded by Trump or a future president. So President Trump has already effected a change to a key element of the Affordable Care Act.

With regard to domestic energy production and repeal of Obama-era environmental policies, Trump issued Executive Order 13783 in late March 2017. This far-reaching order revoked or rescinded one of Obama's executive orders, three presidential memoranda, two presidential reports, and one guidance issued by the Council on Environmental Quality. Perhaps the most significant section of Trump's executive order was the directive that federal agencies "review existing regulations that potentially burden the development or use of domestically produced energy resources and appropriately suspend, revise, or rescind those that unduly burden the development of domestic energy resources beyond the degree necessary to protect the public interest or otherwise comply with the law" (White House 2017). In response to the order, Trump's Environmental Protection Agency (EPA) administrator Scott Pruitt, who had been party to 14 legal challenges to Obama-era EPA rules while Oklahoma's attorney general, announced that the EPA would immediately undertake such a review ("EPA" 2017). There was little doubt that the main target of the executive order was the Clean Power Plan, a regulation issued by the EPA under the

Obama administration, which would require states to dramatically reduce carbon dioxide emissions from power plants by 32 percent below 2005 levels over the next few decades.

Ordinarily, an executive order would not be sufficient to halt a federal regulation, but the Clean Power Plan was never implemented because it was challenged in court by a coalition of Republican-led states (Valdmanis 2017), and the US Supreme Court had issued a stay preventing the plan from going forward. That delay provided an opening for President Trump to upend what would have represented a substantial change to US environmental and energy policy. A coalition of Democrat-led states filed suit, asking the courts to force the Trump administration to comply with the Clean Power Plan regulations, but the Trump administration responded by asking the court to delay any consideration of the legality of the Clean Power Plan until after the EPA had an opportunity to review and revise the plan. In late April 2017 the US Court of Appeals for the District of Columbia granted the administration's request and halted all litigation and consideration of the case for 60 days (Eilperin and Dennis 2017). At the conclusion of the 60 days, the court indicated that the rule would be either remanded to the EPA for review and revision or held in abeyance, meaning enforcement of the Clean Power Plan would remain frozen by the Supreme Court's stay, and the EPA could take its time in considering any next steps. Either outcome is a victory for the Trump administration and a defeat for Obama's policy (Cushman et al. 2017).

Trump also ordered a review of fuel-efficiency standards for vehicles manufactured between 2022 and 2025 put in in place by the Obama administration. Echoing industry sentiment, Trump argued the new standards were too tough on the auto industry. The EPA and the Department of Transportation (DoT) published a fuel economy regulation in 2012 requiring cars built in 2025 to achieve a goal of 54.5 miles per gallon. The EPA had committed to conducting a midterm evaluation of the requirements to determine whether they were still feasible. That evaluation was expected sometime after 2017. Following Trump's surprise victory, the EPA rushed to complete the review before Trump took office. The EPA issued a report affirming the initial goals just days before Trump's inauguration. But the DoT never signed off on the report, giving the Trump administration an opening to revise the rule (Plumer 2017). But the Trump administration is still limited with regard to what can be done about the ultimate goal established by the Obama administration. Because the EPA and DoT established the existing goals via the formal rule-making process established by the EPA, any change to the goals must follow the same process. The Trump administration could relax the time line or make compliance easier, but any change to actual goals must go through the formal rule-making process and any revised goals must be defensible based on sound science and research. In other words, they must demonstrate that the original goals were not reasonable (though they successfully navigated the rule-making process) or that new information justifies a revision. And, of course, any revisions would be subject to legal challenge (Plumer 2017). The Trump administration learned the constraints imposed by the formal rule-making process in July 2017. The EPA had suspended an Obama-era regulation limiting methane emissions from new oil and gas wells. Several groups challenged the delay, and in July the United States Court of Appeals for the District of Columbia Circuit ruled the EPA's decision to delay unreasonable and arbitrary. The court determined that the EPA has the authority to reverse or revise the regulation, but that it must do so by initiating a new rule-making process (Friedman 2017).

In addition to taking on the Clean Power Plan and emissions standards, Trump lifted an Obama-imposed moratorium on coal leasing on federal lands and ordered a review of a 2015 rule issued by the EPA, known as Waters of the United States (WOTUS) rule, which greatly expanded the scope of federal authority over waterways in the United States. The rule placed the EPA in charge of protecting streams and wetlands from pollution and degradation—especially from the runoff produced by mining (Malloy 2015). EPA administrator Scott Pruitt, as Oklahoma attorney general, had sued EPA over the regulation. Revision of the WOTUS rule must follow the APA-mandated public review and comment period, and any proposal will be subject to legal challenge—much as Pruitt had challenged the original rule (Eilperin and Mufson 2017). Coupled with the Clean Power Plan, also a target of Pruitt's legal challenges, Trump said these policies represented a "war on coal" (Park 2017).

Collectively, the policies targeted by Trump were core components of the Obama administration's Climate Action Plan (CAP) announced in 2013. The CAP was established to help the United States meet the goal, set by Obama in 2009, of reducing US greenhouse gas emissions by roughly 17 percent below 2005 levels by 2020. Critics of the CAP argued that the economic costs of the plan far outweighed the benefits, with some suggesting particularly devastating impact on the coal industry (Kreutzer, Loris, and Dayaratna 2013). The Trump White House echoed these sentiments with a statement posted to the White House website, which reads, in part,

"President Trump is committed to eliminating harmful and unnecessary policies such as the Climate Action Plan . . . Lifting these restrictions will greatly help American workers, increasing wages by more than $30 billion over the next 7 years" ("Presidential Executive Order" 2017).

With the stage set for the dismantling of the Climate Action Plan, Trump announced the logical next step in June 2017 when he announced that the United States would withdraw from the Paris Climate Accord. Finalized in 2015, the Paris agreement was signed by 195 nations and was intended to represent a global commitment to combat climate change, especially rising temperatures, by reducing emissions of greenhouse gases. Under Obama, the United States agreed to reduce its greenhouse gas emissions by 26 to 28 percent below 2005 levels by 2025 and to commit up to $3 billion in aid for poorer countries by 2020 (Shear 2017). In withdrawing from the agreement, Trump made good on a frequent campaign promise to do so. Trump was able to unilaterally withdraw the United States from the Paris agreement because it was a nonbinding executive agreement signed by President Obama. Obama understood that the agreement would never receive the two-thirds majority required for treaty ratification in the Senate or even a majority in the House and Senate in support of a resolution affirming the executive agreement, so he bypassed the Congress altogether. The decision to enter into an executive agreement enabled Obama to commit the United States to the goals and obligations of the Paris agreement, but it also meant that the agreement was only as strong as his successor's commitment to it. As President Obama famously scolded Republicans following his 2008 victory, "Elections have consequences" (McCutcheon and Mark 2014).

As a candidate, Donald Trump committed himself to a domestic policy agenda of reduced regulatory burdens and the promotion of greater domestic energy production. Trump's decision to dismantle the Climate Action Plan and withdraw from the Paris agreement, coupled with two presidential memoranda to revive the Dakota and Keystone XL pipelines, halted by President Obama, represented a clear attempt to deliver on that commitment. President Trump was able to take these actions swiftly for a very simple reason: much of President Obama's environmental and energy policy legacy was built on unilateral executive actions—actions that a predecessor could undo. Speaking in 2014, Obama made clear his willingness to go it alone: "I've got a pen to take executive actions where Congress won't" (Keith 2014). A clear early lesson of the Trump presidency is that programs created by the stroke of a pen can often be undone by the stroke of a pen.

But these pen-wielding victories have been confined mostly to Trump policies and actions that are best categorized as unilateral and reactive. Trump has made effective use of the powers afforded the presidency to dismantle policies that Obama created using those same executive powers. As is discussed in chapter 3, Trump has enjoyed success in Congress as well with regard to reactive policies that require congressional action to reverse executive actions. The use of the Congressional Review Act to rescind regulations issued and finalized during the final months of the Obama administration is simply unprecedented. And the wording of the Congressional Review Act makes it difficult for substantively similar regulations to be reissued under a future president. But the number of pending and nonfinal regulations subject to unilateral action is limited. There are no longer any regulations issued by Obama that are susceptible to the Congressional Review Act. President Trump is transitioning to the point in his presidency where his proactive policies, be they unilateral or with Congress, must move to the front of his agenda. But he has struggled in his relations with Congress, and many federal agencies continue to suffer from staff vacancies that limit the ability to revise and review existing policies let alone develop and issue new ones (Uhrmacher 2017). Thus far, Trump has not replicated the first-year success of his recent predecessors with regard to the creation of new initiatives.

STRATEGIC COMPETENCE

It is reasonable, then, to ask, why hasn't Trump replicated the first-year successes of Clinton or Obama? Internal division within the GOP in Congress is discussed in chapter 3 and certainly plays a role. But Clinton and Obama faced ideological divisions within their Democratic majorities as well and overcame them. One possible explanation for the differing level of success may lie in the very different relationships with their party. Trump was an insurgent candidate with no clear link to the Republican Party. During his campaign he ran against the Republican establishment and often distanced himself from or disparaged Republican lawmakers. And many lawmakers responded in kind. This suggests Trump cannot simply rely on unified partisan control of government to pursue his agenda, an agenda that includes policies not readily accepted by many elected Republicans. Trump's difficulties may stem from challenges closer to the Executive Office of the President. As noted, many federal agencies are severely understaffed. Beyond the cabinet secretary, there are hundreds of high-level agency positions that must be nominated by the president and confirmed by the Senate. As of the end of June 2017, only the cabinet secretary had been appointed and approved in 8 of 15 cabinet departments, and by late July Trump had submitted far fewer nominees than either of his two most recent predecessors. These high-level vacancies have placed agency staffing on hold and resulted in significant vacancies at all levels. Administration officials and members of Congress warn that these vacancies imperil the president's policy agenda (Rein 2017). Though the Senate has confirmed Trump nominees at a slower pace than for Bush, Clinton, or Obama, President Trump has submitted far fewer names for confirmation than his immediate predecessors. At his 100-day mark, Trump had forwarded to the Senate fewer than half the number of nominees submitted by Obama during the same time frame.

One explanation for Trump's difficulties may be found via a review of what political scientist Paul Quirk refers to as *strategic competence* (Nelson 2010). As told by Quirk, prevailing models of presidential leadership largely fall into two categories, the self-reliant model and the minimalist model. Under the self-reliant model, a president looks for very little outside help and assumes significant responsibility for all decision making. Such a model requires a substantial degree of skill as well as a clear understanding of how government and policy work. At the very least, it requires the ability to ingest and digest significant amounts of information in order to make decisions. Contrary to the self-reliant model of president leadership is what Quirk refers to as the minimalist model. Under this approach to leadership, presidents are not required to be particularly well versed in specifics of governing or policy but rely instead on the expertise and guidance of experts who serve in the executive branch. Under the minimalist model a president acts very much as a chairman of the board responsible for setting general policies and goals and then delegating responsibility for the specifics to the cabinet and other key players dedicated to the president's vision.

Supposed examples of each approach are evident in prior presidencies. According to Quirk, Franklin Roosevelt is often offered as the quintessential self-reliant president. Roosevelt "made strenuous efforts to ensure his thorough understanding of issues and thus increase his control" (in Nelson 2010, 109). For Roosevelt, this meant establishing competing information sources within his administration and a reliance on sources outside of his administration. Quirk argues that the idea of a self-reliant president who makes major decisions himself and establishes firm control over subordinates has great popular appeal. The minimalist approach requires little specific knowledge on the part of a president, but rather the full and active participation of White House staff and executive branch officers enables a minimalist president to exercise power as expansively as a self-reliant counterpart. President Reagan is often seen as an exemplar of the minimalist model and was described by his spokesman early in his presidency as a chairman of the board who would set broad goals and objectives and then delegate to his cabinet and other key personnel the responsibility of determining specifics.

There are flaws evident in both models of presidential leadership. The self-reliant model tends to understate the immense difficulty inherent in contemporary governing. Simply stated, no single president could be expected to do everything. As Quirk notes, Franklin Roosevelt's commitment to making all key decisions resulted in delays, as there were simply too many decisions to be made. Likewise, presidents who pursue a self-reliant approach are likely to neglect important aspect of their job even as they focus intently on other aspects. In the end, Quirk determines that the self-reliant approach is physically impossible for a modern president.

The minimalist model presents challenges of its own. By delegating responsibility for policy specifics, a minimalist president effectively surrenders control of his goals and objectives and will likely be unable to determine whether a subordinate is making a decision based on the president's goals and objectives or based on those of the subordinate. Quirk (in Nelson 2010, 112) argues as well that a minimalist president is likely to "overestimate his capabilities and judgement" and would not recognize meaningful analysis or accept that others engage in a more sophisticated level of analysis than does the president.

It is quite difficult to apply either model to Donald Trump based on his early actions as president. The evolution of his executive orders restricting travel from several majority Muslim countries highlights this fact. On January 27, 2017, President Trump issued an executive order banning entry to the United States for 90 days by citizens from Iraq, Syria, Iran, Libya, Somalia, Sudan, and Yemen. The order also halted the admission of all refugees from Syria for an indefinite period of time ("Full Text" 2017). In keeping with the self-reliant model, the initial executive order closely approximated pledges made by Trump on the campaign trail. Rather than farming the specific details of the order to professionals with clear knowledge of the potential legal and policy ramifications, the president entrusted the writing to his chief strategist, Stephen Bannon, and policy advisor Stephen Miller. Neither man had any expertise in the area of US immigration policy. Senior personnel within the Department of Homeland Security, the agency that would carry out the order, were not consulted regarding the order. In fact, officials responsible for administering the order were briefed on it at the very moment the president was signing the order (Shear and Nixon 2017). Further, because many of Trump's nominees had yet to be named or confirmed, top officials within the Justice Department—who would be responsible for defending the order against expected legal challenges—were excluded from any review.

Though this process is somewhat consistent with the self-reliant model, it is betrayed by the fact that presidents under this model are said to make every effort to be thoroughly informed about the specifics of each policy. But this does not appear to apply to Trump, according to Trump's own words and officials within his administration. In December 2016 President-elect Trump stated that he did not require the daily intelligence briefings typical of all presidents and presidents-elect (Nelson and Kim 2016), and a classified memo leaked to the press in February 2017 indicated that intelligence briefings delivered to the president were to be kept short and limited to only a few key facts (Beavers 2017). This would appear to support Trump as a minimalist president as opposed to a self-reliant.

But the minimalist model is a poor fit as well. Trump did not act as a chairman of the board in the creation of the travel executive order. He did not entrust its construction to administration officials with the requisite expertise. After the original travel ban was halted by several federal courts, the president issued a revised executive order in March 2017. The new order showed clear evidence of vetting and review by the Justice Department and national security officials and attempted to address many of the issues that resulted in the defeat of the initial order (Zapotosky, Nakamura, and Hauslohner 2017). But Trump's willingness to defer to the others for the development of specifics was short lived. The revised ban was blocked by the federal courts, and in June 2017, following a series of terror attacks in London, Trump took to Twitter to condemn his revised order and the officials who crafted it. Trump tweeted:

"The Justice Dept. should ask for an expedited hearing of the watered down Travel Ban before the Supreme Court—& seek much tougher version!"

"People, the lawyers and the courts can call it whatever they want," Trump wrote on Monday. "But I am calling it what we need and what it is, a TRAVEL BAN!"

Within days of issuing those tweets, the Ninth US Circuit Court of Appeals upheld a lower court ruling to block the order. In the decision, the court cited Trump's tweets as evidence that the order was a blanket ban on travel based on nationality—something prohibited by federal immigration law (Dolan and Kaleem 2017). The US Supreme Court ultimately reinstated key parts of the ban in late June 2017 pending further review by the court in the fall.

It would appear that Trump embodies elements of the minimalist and the self-reliant models. As stated previously, Quirk believed that neither the minimalist nor the self-reliant model were workable. In that respect, it need not be surprising or concerning that Trump is not captured well by either. Quirk presented a third model residing in a gray area between self-reliance and minimalism—the strategic competence model (Nelson 2010). This model requires adoption of a conscious strategy in which a president accepts that his time, energy, and talent represent scarce resources. As a result, strategic decisions need to made regarding what things the president will attempt to know and decide. Given that no president can be expected to know everything, there will be decisions that will be better served by delegation to others and decisions better made by the president. Given the volume and complexity of issues covered by public policy, some degree of presidential ignorance is inevitable. In circumstances where the president is not well versed, it is crucial that he delegates responsibility to skilled and knowledgeable aides who share his philosophy and agenda.

The strategic competence model requires quite a bit from a president. First and foremost a president must be aware of the limits of his own knowledge. Next, a president must make a concerted effort to establish a clear process by which decisions are made and have someone in his inner circle dedicated to protecting that process. Such a process requires that a president impose the restrictions of that process even on himself. Finally, a president must develop a competent process for policy promotion once a decision has been made. Meeting this requirement demands a "fine-grained, practical understanding of how the political institutions work" (Nelson 2010, 121). This need not mean that only presidents with extensive experience can succeed; it simply means that presidents lacking such experience must recognize what they are lacking and hire folks who have the necessary experience.

In late June 2017 the Trump administration demonstrated its struggles with the finer points of politics, law, and institutional relations. The

Presidential Advisory Commission on Voter Integrity, established by President Trump to investigate unsubstantiated claims of widespread voter fraud in the 2016 election, held its first meeting in July 2017 (Bowden 2017). Prior to the meeting, the commission sent a letter to every state requesting both personal and public information from the nation's 200 million voters. In addition to information such as voter names and party affiliation, the commission requested personal information like birth dates, felony conviction records, voting histories, and the last four digits of all voters' Social Security numbers (Wines 2017).

The information request was met with immediate and bipartisan resistance among states. Although Vice President and commission chair Mike Pence told commission members that only publicly available data was being requested, very few states make public all of the information requested, several states have laws prohibiting the sharing of voter information, and the Federal Privacy Act of 1974 prohibits the federal government from collecting much of the information requested. Among the states refusing to fully comply with the request were Indiana, where Vice President Pence had served as governor, and Kansas, where cochair Kris Kobach was secretary of state (Berman and Weigel 2017). Angry over the widespread negative reaction to the data request and state refusals to comply, President Trump took to Twitter to ask, "What are they trying to hide?" (Berman and Weigel 2017), with the answer from many states being that voter information is protected by either state or federal law. In late July, a federal court ruled that the commission's data request did not violate federal privacy protections, but an appeal was planned and many states maintained their unwillingness to cooperate (Haag 2017). Though much of the requested data can be obtained from public sources, the whole affair was an indication that the Trump administration continued to make decisions based on presidential preference with no clear process for vetting or review.

The Trump administration made another strategic error in the midst of the crucial Senate debate over the repeal and replace of the Affordable Care Act in late July. Alaska Senator Lisa Murkowski has been a consistent "no" vote on Senate repeal and replace efforts. When Murkowski voted against a procedural motion to begin debating reform, President Trump lashed out at her via Twitter: "Senator @lisamurkowski of the Great State of Alaska really let the Republicans, and our country, down yesterday. Too bad!" Just hours after the president's tweet, Secretary of the Interior Ryan Zinke called Murkowski and fellow Alaskan Senator Dan Sullivan to warn them that the Trump administration may withhold or reverse support for crucial energy and infrastructure projects in Alaska should Murkowski continue to vote "no" (Chappell 2017). Murkowski, who doesn't stand for reelection until 2022, was undeterred. Perhaps worse for Zinke and the Trump administration, Murkowski chairs both the Senate Committee on Energy and Natural Resources and the Appropriations Committee's subcommittee on the interior—meaning that Murkowski is simultaneously the top authorizer and appropriator for the Department of the Interior. Following the phone call from Zinke, Murkowski postponed a scheduled vote to confirm six of President Trump's nominations for the departments of energy and the interior (Siciliano 2017). This was a fight that Trump did not need and, coupled with his public shaming of Attorney General (and former senator) Jeff Sessions and Senate Majority Leader Mitch McConnell, did nothing to strengthen his working relationship with the Senate.

Trump further complicated matters following a violent August weekend in Charlottesville, Virginia, when a planned protest of the removal of Confederate-era memorials attracted neo-Nazis, white supremacists, and other alt-right groups. The protest quickly descended into violence as protesters and counterprotestors clashed. The events culminated in the death of one counterprotestor and the serious injury of many others when they were struck by a car driven by an apparent white supremacist with Nazi sympathies. Trump's initial response to the events focused on what he saw as the violent acts committed by protestors and counterprotestors. Deemed by many to be an inadequate response, Trump delivered more formal remarks in which he condemned hate groups and their ideologies. However, two days later, at a press conference intended to jump-start Trump's infrastructure agenda, Trump went off script and again decried the violence committed by both sides of the protest and suggested that although there were "very bad people" in the form of neo-Nazis and white supremacists at the protest, "you also had people that were very fine people" protesting with them (Wang and Breuninger 2017).

The backlash that followed these comments overshadowed all of Trump's agenda and created further divisions between Trump and Republicans in Congress. Republican senator Bob Corker (TN) questioned whether Trump had the stability or competence to be an effective president (Herb 2017). In video and images of the press conference, Trump's newly appointed chief of staff John Kelly (who had been brought onboard to increase the message discipline with the White House) could be seen with arms crossed as he stared solemnly at the ground. In the days that followed, multiple CEOs resigned from advisory councils that Trump had established, and Trump was ultimately compelled to disband the councils altogether rather than face more resignations. As the controversy and distraction continued to boil over, it was announced that Steve Bannon, viewed by many as the alt-right point man in the Trump White House and a supporter of Trump's controversial statements, would be leaving the White House (Haberman 2017).

Quirk concludes by arguing that the presidency is not an impossible job; all aspects of the job are ultimately manageable so long as a president has a strategy for competence that makes the best and most effective use of his capabilities—it requires self-discipline, a knowledge of one's limitations and abilities, and a willingness to accept the advice and counsel of those who may hold the expertise that he lacks.

If neither the minimalist nor the self-reliant model fits well with Trump's style, how well does strategic competence fit? At this early stage of his presidency it does not appear to fit very well. Rather than look to seasoned Washington operatives, Donald Trump populated his inner circle of advisors with family members, people he has long known, or those who worked for his campaign. The president appointed Steve Bannon to serve as his chief strategist. Bannon had been a successful investment banker and media executive (in charge of the right-wing news outlet Breitbart) and was the architect of Trump's "America First" campaign strategy. But Bannon had no governing experience and was out of the administration within 8 months. Reince Priebus, the former director of the Republican National Committee, was Trump's first chief of staff. Though Priebus is close friends with Republican House Speaker Paul Ryan, he was largely a Wisconsin political operative with limited meaningful connections in Washington, DC. Chiefs of staff typically serve as gatekeepers determining who could lay claim to a president's limited time. Priebus's brief tenure was tumultuous and marked by a clear lack of discipline in the Oval Office with little control over who had access to the president's ear.

Priebus was replaced by General John Kelly, who had been serving as Trump's director of homeland security. Kelly, a retired United States Marine Corps general and the former commander of United States Southern Command, set an immediate goal of better managing access to the president. Though Kelly is widely respected in Washington, his brief stint as director of homeland security was his first civilian post in government. Jared Kushner, a real estate developer and the president's 36-year-old son-in-law, was named a senior advisor though his areas of policy expertise are unclear. Kellyanne Conway is a well-known Republican pollster who served Vice President Mike Pence in Indiana. Though described as a counselor to the president, her role has largely been one of communicating with the press. The president's daughter Ivanka was appointed special advisor to the president; she previously served as an executive vice president for the Trump Organization before founding a fashion and accessory brand. She has no specific policy expertise or experience. Stephen Miller is a 31-year-old policy advisor who had worked for Senator Jeff Sessions before joining the Trump campaign. Though Miller has some Washington, DC, political experience, he was one of the architects of the original executive order on travel for majority Muslim countries and played a role in not alerting relevant agencies to the content of the order (Krol 2017). Keith Schiller, the director of Oval Office operations, was director of security for the Trump Organization and Donald Trump's bodyguard. Schiller has been described as the most underestimated man in the Trump administration, perhaps having more influence that Reince Priebus (Merica 2017).

Vice President Mike Pence represents the most experienced member of Trump's inner circle and was touted early on as the central figure in Trump's relationship with Congress. In addition to his three years as Indiana governor, Pence served 12 years in the US House of Representatives and enjoys a positive relationship with much of the House leadership. Pence is respected by many Republican members of Congress, understands the legislative process in the House, and has connections with many Republican senators who had served with him in the House. When the Senate is in session, Pence hosts weekly dinners with a small group of senators. Each dinner features a conversation on a different theme or legislative priority (Allen 2017). Pence has emerged as a trusted intermediary in negotiations with the US Congress over key legislative priorities such as the repeal and replace of the Affordable Care Act but has yet to deliver any significant legislative victories.

Collectively, Trump's inner circle was not one established to support a minimalist model of the presidency where a chairman of the board delegates responsibility to experts. Nor does it suit well the strategic competence model, because the inner circle is lacking in personnel with the expertise that the president lacks. Published reports suggest that Trump has grown distrustful of his own staff and has increasingly looked to family members and longtime aides for advice (Pace and Lemire 2017). The process surrounding Trump's decision to fire FBI Director James Comey raises questions as well. Administration officials reported that Trump relied heavily on consultation with family members and Keith Schiller regarding the decision to fire Comey. Lacking the advice and input of those with more political experience, Trump was unprepared for the controversy that followed the firing. Rather than develop a strategy for justifying the decision, the White House Communications Office learned of the firing one hour before it took place. Director Comey learned of his firing from a news report. The Communications Office's ability to justify the firing was hampered by ever-changing explanations coming from the president. The White House initially said the firing was the result of recommendations from the attorney general and the assistant attorney general. In an interview with NBC News, President Trump contradicted that argument by suggesting that he had intended to fire Comey regardless of the recommendations of the Justice Department. As the Communications Office faced ever more difficulty presenting a consistent explanation for the firing, Trump reportedly decided that he was the one who needed to be in charge of the communications strategy and the only effective spokesperson for his administration (Pace and Lemire 2017).

Those who have known and worked with Trump for a long time make clear that he takes a collaborative approach to management and values the advice and input of others when making decisions. But, and this is key, Trump is said to seek the advice and input of those he trusts despite their expertise (Merica 2017). Strategic competence demands that a president look to those with expertise on matters the president knows less about. President Reagan, who lacked a deep understanding of many policy areas and felt no obligation to become an expert in everything, looked to experts who could guide his agenda even if that meant selecting staff who had served his political adversaries. Reagan's first chief of staff, James Baker, had served President Gerald Ford—Reagan's rival for the 1976 Republican nomination for president—and advised George Bush, another Reagan rival, in the 1980 battle for the Republican nomination. But Baker was a gifted organizer who understood the value of process and knew how the system worked (Nelson 2010). Reagan's reliance on staff with knowledge and experience resulted in a very successful first year in office despite divided control of Congress. Bill Clinton, by contrast, staffed his White House with campaign loyalists and folks who had served him as governor of Arkansas. Clinton's first chief of staff, Mack McClarty, was a longtime friend and successful businessman who had no political experience. As a result, Clinton's first year in office was marred by indications of disarray and poor management. Clinton made poor use of his time as he engaged in lengthy policy discussions with his staff; yet there were often no clear indications as to why certain decisions were made. Clinton took corrective action in his second year by bringing a seasoned DC politico, Leon Panetta, as his chief of staff and hiring a successful advisor to Republican presidents, David Gergen, as a strategist (Nelson 2010).

BOLD PROMISES AND HARSH REALITIES

In a speech delivered in Gettysburg in October 2016, Donald Trump unveiled an ambitious domestic policy agenda and made the bold promise of acting on most of it within his first 100 days in office. Consistent with the themes of this chapter, some of his promises were reactive and others proactive. Some of his promises could be accomplished unilaterally while others would require congressional action. Education reform, health-care reform, tax reform, immigration reform, and modernizing America's aging infrastructure all occupy a spot on Trump's agenda, and none can be accomplished without Congress. As discussed in chapter 3, much of his proactive agenda requires Congress, and accomplishments have been minimal.

Trump's pledge to roll back President Obama's regulatory legacy has enjoyed greater success, especially in the initial months of his presidency. The effectiveness with which the White House and the Republican Congress worked to identify regulations to reverse using the Congressional Review Act shows that a disciplined focus is possible. Much of the effort was led by a small team of White House staff and key members of Congress, demonstrating the very strategic competence that the president's proactive agenda requires. But repealing recent regulations with the CRA and delaying or revising regulations that were yet to be finalized is essentially picking the low-hanging fruit. The decision by the United States Court of Appeals for the District of Columbia Circuit to block the EPA from halting President Obama's methane regulations hints at the challenges that await the remaining, and more substantive, items on Trump's domestic agenda.

Thus far, Trump's first year in office resembles more the disarray of Clinton's initial year than it does the success of Reagan's. But it is important to point out that Reagan never enjoyed another year as successful as his first, at least with regard to domestic policy, and Clinton's successes came after his initial troubles and his decision to restructure the White House staff. The key for Trump, and what may determine whether he is able to successfully pursue his proactive policy agenda, is whether he is willing to accept the limits of his own knowledge and skills and place as much value on expertise as he does on trust and loyalty among the staff and advisors that he turns to when decisions must be made.

WORKS CITED

Allen, Mike. "Pence's 'Polite Distance' from Trump." Axios. July 2, 2017. Accessed July 3, 2017. https://www.axios.com/pences-polite-distance-from -trump-2451998474.html.

"An America First Energy Plan." The White House. March 8, 2017. Accessed June 28, 2017. https://www.whitehouse.gov/america-first-energy.

Associated Press. "Obama: If Congress Won't Act I Will." *Newsday*. October 31, 2011. Accessed June 27, 2017. http://www.newsday.com/news/nation/obama -if-congress-won-t-act-i-will-1.3287261.

Beavers, Olivia. "Classified Memo Tells Intel Officials to Keep Trump's Daily Brief-ings Short: Report." *The Hill*. February 16, 2017. Accessed June 19, 2017. http:// thehill.com/blogs/blog-briefing-room/news/319847-classified-memo-tells -intel-officials-to-keep-trumps-daily.

Berman, Mark, and David Weigel. "Trump's Voting Commission Asked States to Hand Over Election Data. Some Are Pushing Back." *Washington Post*. July 1, 2017. Accessed July 2, 2017. https://www.washingtonpost.com/national/ trumps-voting-commission-asked-states-to-hand-over-election-data-theyre -pushing-back/2017/06/30/cd8f812a-5dce-11e7-9b7d-14576dc0f39d_story .html?utm_term=.be3f021de25b.

Bowden, John. "Trump's Election Integrity Commission Will Meet for First Time in July." *The Hill*. June 28, 2017. Accessed July 2, 2017. http://thehill. com/homenews/administration/339923-pence-prepares-for-first-meeting-of -election-integrity-commission.

Chappell, Bill. "After Trump Targets Murkowski, Interior Secretary Reportedly Warns Alaska's Senators." NPR. July 27, 2017. Accessed August 22, 2017. http://www.npr.org/sections/thetwo-way/2017/07/27/539765891/after-trump -targets-murkowski-interior-secretary-reportedly-warns-alaskas-senato.

Cohen, Marshall, and Wade Payson-Denney. "By the Numbers: How Trump Stacks Up after 100 Days." CNN. May 1, 2017. Accessed June 26, 2017. http:// edition.cnn.com/2017/04/29/politics/donald-trump-100-days-data/index.html.

Cooper, Phillip J. *By Order of the President: The Use and Abuse of Executive Direct Action*. Lawrence: University Press of Kansas, 2014.

Crews, Clydes. "Obama's Legacy: An Abundance of Executive Actions." *Forbes*. January 10, 2016. Accessed July 8, 2017. https://www.forbes.com/ sites/waynecrews/2016/01/10/this-inventory-of-obamas-dozens-of-executive -actions-frames-his-final-state-of-the-union-address/#401106a875f5.

Cushman, John H., Jr., Phil McKenna, Leslie Kaufman, Bob Berwyn, Nicholas Kusnetz, Georgina Gustin, Marianne Lavelle, and Zahra Hirji. "Here's What to Know about the Latest Legal Showdown over Obama's Clean Power Plan." Inside Climate News. May 17, 2017. Accessed June 27, 2017. https://inside climatenews.org/news/16052017/clean-power-plan-epa-lawsuit-trump-obama -climate-change.

Dolan, Maura, and Jaweed Kaleem. "U.S. 9th Circuit Court of Appeals Refuses to Reinstate Trump's Travel Ban." *Los Angeles Times*. June 12, 2017. Accessed June 19, 2017. http://www.latimes.com/local/lanow/la-na-9thcircuit-travel-ban -20170530-story.html.

Eilperin, Juliet, and Brady Dennis. "Court Freezes Clean Power Plan Lawsuit, Signaling Likely End to Obama's Signature Climate Policy." *Washington Post*. April 28, 2017. Accessed June 27, 2017. https://www.washingtonpost .com/news/energy-environment/wp/2017/04/28/court-freezes-clean-power -plan-lawsuit-signaling-likely-end-to-obamas-signature-climate-policy/?utm_ term=.0348d379fd8d.

Eilperin, Juliet, and Steven Mufson. "Federal Court Blocks Trump EPA on Air Pollution." *Washington Post*. July 3, 2017. Accessed August 22, 2017. https://www.washingtonpost.com/politics/federal-court-blocks-trump-epa-on -air-pollution/2017/07/03/464a7344-601e-11e7-84a1-a26b75ad39fe_story .html?utm_term=.b75d42c0285d.

"EPA to Review the Clean Power Plan Under President Trump's Executive Or-der." EPA. March 28, 2017. Accessed June 27, 2017. https://www.epa.gov/news releases/epa-review-clean-power-plan-under-president-trumps-executive-order.

"Executive Order Minimizing the Economic Burden of the Patient Protection and Affordable Care Act Pending Repeal." The White House. January 23, 2017. Ac-cessed June 27, 2017. https://www.whitehouse.gov/the-press-office/2017/01/2/ executive-order-minimizing-economic-burden-patient-protection-and.

Friedman, Lisa. "Court Blocks E.P.A. Effort to Suspend Obama-Era Methane Rule." *New York Times*. July 3, 2017. Accessed July 4, 2017. https://www.nytimes .com/2017/07/03/climate/court-blocks-epa-effort-to-suspend-obama-era-meth ane-rule.html.

"Full Text of Trump's Executive Order on 7-Nation Ban, Refugee Suspension." CNN. January 28, 2017. Accessed June 19, 2017. http://www.cnn.com/2017/01/28/ politics/text-of-trump-executive-order-nation-ban-refugees/index.html.

Goldstein, Amy. "Aetna Exiting All ACA Insurance Marketplaces in 2018." *Wash-ington Post*. May 10, 2017. Accessed June 27, 2017. https://www.washington post.com/national/health-science/aetna-exiting-all-aca-insurance-marketplaces -in-2018/2017/05/10/9dedbeea-35d4-11e7-b373-418f6849a004_story.html.

Haag, Matthew. "Judge Clears Way for Trump's Voter Fraud Panel to Collect Data." *New York Times*. July 24, 2017. Accessed August 22, 2017. https://www .nytimes.com/2017/07/24/us/politics/trump-voter-fraud-panel.html?mcubz=1.

Haberman, Maggie. "Trump Tells Aides He Has Decided to Remove Stephen Bannon." *New York Times*. August 18, 2017. Accessed August 18, 2017. https://www.nytimes.com/2017/08/18/us/politics/steve-bannon-trump-white-house.html.

Herb, Jeremy. "Corker: Trump Hasn't Demonstrated the Stability or Competence to Be Successful." CNN. August 18, 2017. Accessed August 18, 2017. http://www.cnn.com/2017/08/17/politics/bob-corker-criticizes-trump-charlottesville/index.html.

Keith, Tamara. "Wielding a Pen and a Phone, Obama Goes It Alone." NPR. January 20, 2014. Accessed June 28, 2017. http://www.npr.org/2014/01/20/263766043/wielding-a-pen-and-a-phone-obama-goes-it-alone.

Kessler, Glenn. "Claims Regarding Obama's Use of Executive Orders and Presidential Memoranda." *Washington Post*. December 31, 2014. Accessed June 30, 2017. https://www.washingtonpost.com/news/fact-checker/wp/2014/12/31/claims-regarding-obamas-use-of-executive-orders-and-presidential-memoranda/?utm_term=.37c3e90229d5.

Kopan, Tal. "Can Trump Reverse Obama's Regulations on 'Day One'?" CNN. September 28, 2016. Accessed June 20, 2017. http://www.cnn.com/2016/09/28/politics/trump-executive-action-obama/index.html.

Kopan, Tal. "Trump Puts Freeze on New Regulations." CNN. January 20, 2017. Accessed July 1, 2017. http://edition.cnn.com/2017/01/20/politics/reince-priebus-regulations-memo/index.html.

Kreutzer, David, Nicolas Loris, and Kevin Dayaratna. "EPA Power Plant Regulations: A Backdoor Energy Tax." Heritage Foundation. December 5, 2013. Accessed August 22, 2017. http://www.heritage.org/environment/report/epa-power-plant-regulations-backdoor-energy-tax.

Krol, Our Foreign Staff; Charlotte. "Donald Trump's Inner Circle: Who Are the Key Figures Driving the President's Policy Agenda?" *The Telegraph*. February 2, 2017. Accessed June 19, 2017. http://www.telegraph.co.uk/news/0/donald-trumps-inner-circle-key-figures-driving-presidents-policy/.

Lehmann, Evan, and Nathanael Massey. "Obama Warns Congress to Act on Climate Change, or He Will." *Scientific American*. February 13, 2013. Accessed June 27, 2017. https://www.scientificamerican.com/article/obama-warns-congress-to-act-on-climate-change-or-he-will/.

Malloy, Allie. "Obama Announces New EPA Protection of Waterways." CNN. May 27, 2015. Accessed June 28, 2017. http://edition.cnn.com/2015/05/27/politics/obama-epa-water-rule/.

McCutcheon, Chuck, and David Mark. "'Elections Have Consequences': Does Obama Regret Saying That Now?" *Christian Science Monitor*. November 21, 2014. Accessed July 2, 2017. https://www.csmonitor.com/USA/Politics/Politics-Voices/2014/1121/Elections-have-consequences-Does-Obama-regret-saying-that-now.

McMinn, Sean. "Graphic: How Presidents Have Used Executive Orders in Their First 100 Days." *Roll Call*. January 24, 2017. Accessed June 26, 2017. http://www.rollcall.com/news/policy/graphic-how-presidents-have-used-executive-orders-in-their-first-100-days.

Merica, Dan. "Meet the 'Most Underestimated Person on Trump's Team.'" CNN. April 16, 2017. Accessed June 19, 2017. http://www.cnn.com/2017/04/16/politics/donald-trump-keith-schiller-security/index.html.

Nelson, Louis, and Seung Min Kim. "Trump: I Don't Need Daily Briefings." *Politico*. December 11, 2016. Accessed June 19, 2017. http://www.politico.com/story/2016/12/trump-briefings-232479.

Nelson, Michael. *The Presidency and the Political System*. Washington, DC: CQ Press, 2010.

Pace, Julie, and Jonathan Lemire. "Trump's Inner Circle Is Rapidly Shrinking." Business Insider. May 13, 2017. Accessed June 19, 2017. http://www.businessinsider.com/trump-inner-circle-is-rapidly-shrinking-2017-5.

Park, Madison. "6 Obama Climate Policies That Trump Orders Change." CNN. March 28, 2017. Accessed August 22, 2017. http://www.cnn.com/2017/03/28/politics/climate-change-obama-rules-trump/index.html.

Pender, Kathleen. "Quiet IRS Change Could Undermine Obamacare, Supporters Say." *San Francisco Chronicle*. February 14, 2017. Accessed June 27, 2017. http://www.sfchronicle.com/business/networth/article/Quiet-IRS-change-could-undermine-Obamacare-10932798.php.

Pfeiffer, Dan. "We Can't Wait." National Archives and Records Administration. October 24, 2011. Accessed June 27, 2017. https://obamawhitehouse.archives.gov/blog/2011/10/24/we-cant-wait.

Plumer, Brad. "Trump's New Plan to Roll Back Obama's Fuel Economy Rules for Cars, Explained." Vox. March 15, 2017. Accessed June 27, 2017. https://www.vox.com/energy-and-environment/2017/3/15/14828070/trump-fuel-economy-standards.

"Presidential Executive Order on Promoting Energy Independence and Economic Growth." The White House. March 28, 2017. Accessed June 27, 2017. https://www.whitehouse.gov/the-press-office/2017/03/28/presidential-executive-order-promoting-energy-independence-and-economi-1.

"Pruitt v. EPA: 14 Challenges of EPA Rules by the Oklahoma Attorney General." *New York Times*. January 14, 2017. Accessed July 2, 2017. https://www.nytimes.com/interactive/2017/01/14/us/politics/document-Pruitt-v-EPA-a-Compilation-of-Oklahoma-14.html.

Rein, Lisa. "Slow Pace of Trump Nominations Leaves Cabinet Agencies 'Stuck' in Staffing Limbo." *Washington Post*. April 25, 2017. Accessed July 1, 2017. https://www.washingtonpost.com/politics/slow-pace-of-trump-nominations-leaves-cabinet-agencies-stuck-in-staffing-limbo/2017/04/25/0a150aba-252c-11e7-b503-9d616bd5a305_story.html.

Schier, Steven E., and Todd E. Eberly. *American Government and Popular Discontent: Stability without Success*. New York: Routledge, 2013.

Shear, Michael D. "Trump Will Withdraw US from Paris Climate Agreement." *New York Times*. June 1, 2017. Accessed June 28, 2017. https://www.nytimes .com/2017/06/01/climate/trump-paris-climate-agreement.html.

Shear, Michael D., and Ron Nixon. "How Trump's Rush to Enact an Immigration Ban Unleashed Global Chaos." *New York Times*. January 29, 2017. Accessed June 19, 2017. https://www.nytimes.com/2017/01/29/us/politics/donald-trump -rush-immigration-order-chaos.html?smid=pl-share&mtrref=www.abajournal .com.

Siciliano, John. "Lisa Murkowski Delays Votes on Trump's Nominees after Threatening Phone Call." *Washington Examiner*. July 27, 2017. Accessed August 12, 2017. http://www.washingtonexaminer.com/lisa-murkowski-delays -votes-on-trumps-nominees-after-threatening-phone-call/article/2629904.

Thurber, James A., and Jordan Tama, eds. *Rivals for Power: Presidential-Congressional Relations*. 6th ed. Lanham, MD: Rowman & Littlefield, 2017.

Uhrmacher, Kevin. "Analysis | Half of Trump's Major Federal Agencies Still Only Have One Senate-Confirmed Appointee." *Washington Post*. June 27, 2017. Accessed July 1, 2017. https://www.washingtonpost.com/news/the-fix/wp/2017/06/27/the-appointee-situation-at-the-state-department-is-bad-these -other-agencies-might-have-it-worse/.

Valdmanis, Richard. "States Challenge Trump over Clean Power Plan." *Scientific American*. April 6, 2017. Accessed August 22, 2017. https://www.scientificam erican.com/article/states-challenge-trump-over-clean-power-plan/.

Wang, Christine, and Christine Breuninger. "Read the Transcript of Donald Trump's Jaw-Dropping Press Conference." CNBC. August 15, 2017. Accessed August 18, 2017. https://www.cnbc.com/2017/08/15/read-the-transcript-of -donald-trumps-jaw-dropping-press-conference.html.

Wines, Michael. "Asked for Voters' Data, States Give Trump Panel a Bipartisan 'No.'" *New York Times*. June 30, 2017. Accessed July 2, 2017. https://www .nytimes.com/2017/06/30/us/politics/kris-kobach-states-voter-fraud-data.html.

Zapotosky, Matt, David Nakamura, and Abigail Hauslohner. "Revised Executive Order Bans Travelers from Six Muslim-Majority Countries from Getting New Visas." *Washington Post*. March 6, 2017. Accessed June 19, 2017. https://www.washingtonpost.com/world/national-security/new-executive -order-bans-travelers-from-six-muslim-majority-countries-applying-for-visas/ 2017/03/06/3012a42a-0277-11e7-ad5b-d22680e18d10_story.html?utm_term= .d8eb898f08b3.

5

Trump's Foreign Policy

@realDonaldTrump
In trade, military and EVERYTHING else, it will be AMERICA
FIRST! This will quickly lead to our ultimate goal: MAKE AMER-
ICA GREAT AGAIN!
(8:46 a.m., May 23, 2016)

During his campaign for the presidency, Donald Trump took a variety of shifting positions about foreign policy challenges facing the nation. But one thing never changed: his encompassing campaign slogans of "America First" and "Make America Great Again." For him, America was always "losing" by engaging in unfair trade deals, failing to restrict illegal immigration, and acting as the world's policeman while other nations failed to adequately fund their own defense.

Trump's foreign policy positions during the 2016 campaign involved frequent improvisation. One example of his changing views concerned whether the United States should accept refugees from war-torn Syria. In September 2015, Trump said "yes" in a Fox News interview: "I hate the concept of it, but on a humanitarian basis, you have to. It's living in hell in Syria. There's no question about it. They're living in hell, and something has to be done." Less than a month later, the answer on Fox News was "no": "I tell you, if they come into this country, they're going out. If I win, they're going out. We can't take a chance." By December,

Trump had gone further, calling for a complete shutdown of all Muslim immigration to the United States (Berenson 2016). Candidate Trump had no governmental experience and a lot to learn about foreign policy. As he gradually gained governmental experience and knowledge as president, several of his foreign policy views underwent change.

What did "America First" and "Make America Great Again" connote during the 2016 campaign? His approach started with a harsh critique of foreign policy in recent decades, particularly under Barack Obama. To Trump, Obama's foreign policy was a "disaster." In an April 27, 2016, speech he identified five major foreign policy shortcomings. The Obama approach (1) overextended military resources that Obama had underfunded, (2) allowed our allies to not pay their fair share for defense, (3) caused our allies to begin to believe they can't rely on us, (4) resulted in our adversaries no longer respecting the United States, and (5) continued the unclear foreign policy that began with the breakup of the Soviet Union in 1989.

In contrast, Trump promised to significantly boost military spending, demand allies pay more for their defense, demonstrate more consistent support for allies (including Israel and eastern European nations), adopt more aggressive policies toward China and North Korea, and create a more coherent foreign policy based on "American interests and the shared interests of our allies" (Beckwith 2016).

Trump framed most of his campaign discussion of foreign policy as a series of harsh disparagements of Obama and Hillary Clinton. His alternative, as the above summary indicates, was briefly summarized in a few attractive but vague principles. Trump's foreign policy approach achieved more definition when he discussed two issues particularly important to the candidate: trade and immigration.

In 2016, Trump constantly asserted that America was a big loser in international trade agreements. In a campaign speech in Pennsylvania, he asserted, "We allowed foreign countries to subsidize their goods, devalue their currencies, violate their agreements and cheat in every way imaginable, and our politicians did nothing about it." His list of disasters included the North American Free Trade Agreement promoted by Bill Clinton and approved by Congress in 1994, allowing China to enter the World Trade Organization (WTO) in 2001, and Obama and Hillary Clinton's toleration of Chinese currency manipulation. For Trump, NAFTA was "the worst trade deal in history." Fifty thousand US factories have shuttered since China entered the WTO. Obama's proposed Trans-Pacific Partnership

(TPP) with twelve Asian nations was another trade giveaway: "It will undermine our economy. It will undermine our independence." Trump's solution? Better negotiated agreements supervised by the author of *The Art of the Deal* (*Time* Staff 2016).

The candidate was equally emphatic about the need for new restrictions on immigration, making it a central theme of his campaign. In August 2015 he announced a sweeping set of policy proposals. He planned to build a wall on the Mexican border, make Mexico pay for it, deport criminal aliens, enhance penalties for overstaying visas, triple the number of ICE (Department of Homeland Security Immigration and Custom Enforcement) officers, pause immigration to help unemployed Americans find jobs, and reduce the number of visas for foreign workers. By November 2015, he had proposed a "deportation force" to remove the approximately 11 million undocumented aliens. Then followed months of varying statements in which he qualified his support for various aspects of his announced plan. By Election Day 2016, Trump maintained his desire to deport many undocumented aliens and to build a border wall paid for by Mexico but had not ruled out a pathway to citizenship for some undocumented aliens (Timm 2017).

Trump's stances on trade and immigration proved very controversial during the 2016 campaign. The US Chamber of Commerce, long supportive of GOP candidates, criticized Trump on trade on the day he gave a speech on that topic in Ohio and Pennsylvania, two states that had lost jobs to foreign competition. The Chamber countered Trump's trade restrictionism, claiming "the benefits of trade greatly outweigh the costs. . . . the vast majority of Americans benefit from international trade and investment" (Murphy 2016). During the fall campaign, Democratic nominee Hillary Clinton accused Trump of "a decades-long record of divisiveness and campaign of hate by pledging to forcibly remove every single undocumented immigrant from our country," terming Trump's vision "one in which immigrants are not welcomed and one in which innocent families are torn apart" (Hensch 2016).

THE TRUMP ADMINISTRATION'S INITIAL IMMIGRATION AND TRADE POLICIES

A week after the inauguration, the Trump administration embroiled itself in a series of political and judicial controversies surrounding its first executive order restricting immigration. Labeled by its critics a "Muslim ban," the order, titled "Protecting the Nation from Foreign Terrorist Entry into the United States," took immediate effect to bar admission to the US of all people with nonimmigrant or immigrant visas from seven countries—Iraq, Syria, Somalia, Iran, Libya, Sudan, and Yemen—for 90 days. It also barred entry to all refugees from anywhere in the world for 120 days and placed an indefinite ban on refugees from war-torn Syria. It prioritized refugees from these countries if they were subject to "religious based persecution" (probably Christians). The ban initially also applied to individuals who are permanent residents of the United States (green-card holders) who were traveling overseas to visit family or for work, though criticism caused the White House immediately to suspend that provision. The order was formulated by White House aides Steve Bannon and Steve Miller. It was not examined or approved by the Departments of Homeland Security, State, or Defense (McGraw and Kelsey 2017).

The executive order stated, "Recent history shows that some of those who have entered the United States through our immigration system have proved to be threats to our national security. Since 2001, hundreds of persons born abroad have been convicted of terrorism-related crimes in the United States . . . the entry into the United States of foreign nationals who may commit, aid, or support acts of terrorism remains a matter of grave concern" (White House 2017a).

The peremptory issuance of the order produced some disarray at airports and strong criticism from congressional Democrats and Republicans. GOP Senators Lindsey Graham (SC) and John McCain (AZ) called the executive order a "self-inflicted wound" that "may do more to help terrorist recruitment than improve our security." Senate Minority Leader Charles Schumer (D-NY) demanded Trump rescind the "mean spirited and un-American" order. In New York, Massachusetts, Virginia, and Washington federal lawsuits were filed for travelers who were detained in US airports (McGraw and Kelsey 2017). By the next day, January 28, a federal judge in New York had issued a temporary ban on the order as the litigation commenced and political resistance mounted. Subsequent attempts by the administration to remove judicial bans on the initial executive order were not successful.

Despite the president's statement on January 29 that the ban "is not about religion—this is about terror and keeping our country safe," ex-president Obama the next day criticized the ban, responding that he "fundamentally disagrees with the notion of discriminating against individuals because of their faith or religion" (Almasy and Simon 2017). The judicial impasse prompted the Trump administration on March 6 to withdraw the initial order and replace it with a new order titled "Protecting the Nation from Foreign Terrorist Entry into the United States." The new order differed from the January 27 order in several ways. It more clearly stated which travelers were subject to the travel ban, removed Iraq from the list of countries, no longer banned Syrian refugees indefinitely, did not rank Christians as refugees having higher priority, allowed the secretaries of state and homeland security to grant exemptions on a case-by-case basis, and required the Departments of Justice and Homeland Security to create a longer chronological list of terror attacks and convictions dating back to September 11, 2001 (Neuhauser 2017).

This order also was stopped by judicial challenges. A federal judge in Hawaii on March 15 issued a restraining order against the ban, arguing that "there was significant and unrebutted evidence of religious animus driving the promulgation" of the order and that "a reasonable, objective observer . . . would conclude" that the ban "was issued with a purpose to disfavor a particular religion" (McGraw and Kelsey 2017). A series of Trump administration defeats in federal circuit courts of appeals ensued, overruling the ban on constitutional or statutory grounds. The Ninth Circuit blocked the ban on *statutory* grounds, holding that Trump "exceeded the scope of the authority delegated to him by Congress" (Stern 2017a). The Fourth Circuit, in an unusual interpretation, looked to Trump's campaign statements on immigration to find an unconstitutional religious intolerance in the ban. Its majority opinion stated that the ban "drips with religious intolerance, animus, and discrimination," thereby violating "one of our most cherished founding principles—that government shall not establish any religious orthodoxy, or favor or disfavor one religion over another" (Stern 2017b). The administration appealed the Fourth Circuit reversal to the Supreme Court, which has ultimate jurisdiction over the judicial controversy (Jarrett and de Vogue 2017).

In preliminary rulings, the Supreme Court gave the Trump administration a partial victory. On June 29 it allowed temporary implementation of the revised ban but expanded the range of people who could be admitted. The court allowed entry to persons having "any bona fide relationship with a person or entity in the United States." In early July the court issued a brief order indicating the Trump administration had interpreted its June 29 ruling too narrowly (de Vogue 2017). The court planned a more comprehensive consideration of the executive order later in the year.

The White House engendered great controversy with its travel ban. After six months in office, it had achieved some limited success in implementing it despite widespread criticism and a pending Supreme Court case. The ban was shaped as a temporary set of restrictions; yet the controversy now extended many days beyond the 120-day scope of much of the original order. The underlying debate, pitting concerns about national security against fears of religious discrimination, will persist well into the future because it surrounds many antiterrorism security measures.

Trump's Department of Homeland Security announced enhanced immigration enforcement policies on February 1. The new policies broadened "the pool of undocumented immigrants" prioritized for removal, including those who have been charged with crimes but not convicted, those who commit acts that constitute a "chargeable criminal offense," and those who an immigration officer concludes pose "a risk to public safety or national security" (Nakamura 2017). One result was an outcry from immigrant rights groups. A senior departmental spokesperson, however, stated, "We do not have the personnel, time or resources to go into communities and round up people and do all kinds of mass throwing folks on buses. That's entirely a figment of folks' imagination. This is not intended to produce mass roundups, mass deportations" (Nakamura 2017).

Meanwhile, Trump claimed in March that illegal border crossings from Mexico had dropped considerably. Did the arrival of his administration produce this result? According to Christopher Wilson, deputy director of the Mexico Institute at the Wilson Center:

> There's been a clear and marked decrease in unauthorized border crossings. That's really undeniable. How much of that is due to policy changes versus rhetoric? It's not really easy to answer that question. My sense is that what we've really seen so far, the big change, has been around rhetoric, communicating. It's been about messaging, and that's worked, essentially. Potential migrants are convinced that this is a difficult time to come to the United States, and they have not been coming. (Lee 2017)

On January 27, Mexican President Enrique Peña Nieto canceled an upcoming meeting with Trump over the president's insistence that Mexico fund the "border wall." Funding for Trump's wall in late April became ensnared in harsh partisan divisions surrounding a must-pass spending bill to temporarily fund the national government. An administration request for wall funding encountered harsh Democratic opposition and was jettisoned from the final legislation. Democrats were able to prevail because the congressional GOP was internally divided on spending and could not muster enough votes to pass the funding with funds for the border wall in it.

When the administration announced its fiscal year 2018 budget proposal on May 22, it requested $2.6 billion for border wall construction and enhanced immigration security. This was a small fraction of the tens of billions needed to fulfill Trump's promise of a border along the entire 1,989-mile border. Though the president asked for 10,000 new immigration (ICE) officers and 5,000 new Border Patrol agents, the 2018 budget would fund only 500 new Border Patrol agents and 1,000 new ICE officers. The White House also requested $1.5 billion to increase detentions and deportations of undocumented immigrants by funding detention and removal efforts. Congressional prospects for approval were uncertain (Kopan 2017). The limited request reflected the austerity of many administration funding requests in the proposal due to the large projected deficit and the administration's desire for a big tax cut.

The administration's initial approach to international trade started with an expected withdrawal from the Trans-Pacific Partnership negotiations and agreement. The agreement negotiated by the Obama administration sought to reduce trade barriers among the United States and 11 Asian nations. One goal of the agreement was to enhance trade with Asian nations other than with China, which was not included in the agreement. Trump called his action "a great deal for the American worker." Richard Trumka, head of the AFL-CIO union federation, 2016 Democratic presidential candidate Bernie Sanders (I-VT), House Democrat Pelosi (CA), and other liberal Democrats hailed the move. Critics included Senator John McCain (R-AZ), who called the action a "serious mistake" (Bennett 2017).

Trump's campaign criticism of the People's Republic of China regarding trade policies and currency manipulation temporarily vanished once Trump met with Chinese President Xi in early April. Trump indicated that he now understood the difficulties China has in dealing with the rogue regime in North Korea. The need for Chinese help with the matter meant he would not bring immediate pressure on trade and currency issues. "They're not currency manipulators," he said on April 17, contradicting earlier campaign assertions (Murphy 2017). Yet by the summer the president was threatening China with trade reprisals in part because of what he viewed as its inaction with the growing North Korea crisis.

The president did, however, indicate his intent to renegotiate the North American Free Trade Agreement, signaling a desire to revisit many aspects of the pact in order to, in his view, improve America's status in the agreement. Up for renegotiation were current trade barriers, agricultural rules, customs enforcement, and dispute resolution procedures. US Trade Representative Robert Lighthizer would lead the negotiations for the United States (Lu 2017).

TRUMP AND THE WORLD

During his presidential campaign, Donald Trump promised a major re-configuration of the nation's foreign policy. He expressed controversial positions on a variety of world trouble spots, military engagements, and diplomatic controversies. During his administration's initial months, Trump clarified and altered many of his previous positions, often at the behest of his foreign and defense policy team. What follows is a tour Trump's evolving positions regarding these world situations as he began conducting the nation's foreign policy.

North Korea and Asian Affairs

In early 2016, candidate Trump viewed the government of North Korea quite negatively and expected China to take control of the North Korean regime. In a February GOP debate, he asserted, "China says they don't have that good of control over North Korea. They have tremendous control. . . . They have total, absolute control, practically, of North Korea. . . . I would get on with China, let China solve that problem. They can do it quickly and surgically. That's what we should do with North Korea" (Team Fix 2016). He later suggested that China should "disappear" North Korean leader Kim Jong Un (CBS News 2016). Trump would revise his approach upon taking office.

As he left the presidency, Barack Obama informed Donald Trump that the most urgent problem he would face was North Korea's attempts to build intercontinental ballistic missiles. Obama's administration led a "cyber war" against North Korea's missile program as a number of the na-tion's test missiles failed to launch successfully (Sanger and Broad 2017). Signs soon appeared after inauguration day that North Korea was planning more missile tests. Trump's options were limited. The United States could continue an intensified cyber and electronic warfare begun under Obama, attempt to reopen negotiations that had yielded little in the past, prepare for missile strikes on launch facilities that promise uncertain results, or encourage China to more aggressively pressure North Korea to desist (Sanger and Broad 2017).

Ten days after his election victory, Trump had met with Japanese Prime Minister Shinzo Abe to discuss a wide variety of issues, including North Korea. The two nations continued working to curtail the North Korean threat. On February 5, the two nations launched a successful antiballistic missile test. Six days later, however, North Korea announced a successful launch of a new ballistic missile, and on February 14 North Korean agents reportedly assassinated Kim Jong Un's half brother in Singapore. China then announced it was suspending all exports of coal to North Korea for the remainder of the year (McKirdy 2017).

The tit for tat with North Korea continued for the next several months. North Korea fired four ballistic test missiles into the Sea of Japan on March 2. This led to the United States dispatching missile defense ships to the area later in the month. Evidence mounted of continued nuclear weapons tests by North Korea, and two unsuccessful ballistic missile launches occurred in March and April. The rogue nation was conducting missile and nuclear tests at its most rapid pace ever.

President Trump met with Chinese President Xi in early April and revised his views regarding China's influence over North Korea. "After listening for 10 minutes, I realized it's not so easy. I felt pretty strongly that they had a tremendous power over North Korea. But it's not what you would think" (Osborne 2017). The North Korean issue again arose at the United Nations Security Council on April 19. Russia vetoed a resolution condemning the most recent nuclear test as a violation of international arms control accords.

Trump then tried a diplomatic overture on May 1, indicating he would be "honored" to meet with Kim Jong Un in direct one-to-one talks. Moon Jae-in, newly elected as president of South Korea on May 10, advocated engagement with the North in order to denuclearize the Korean peninsula. North Korea responded with three ballistic missile launches in May and one in early June. Its first successful tests of intercontinental ballistic missiles came in July, raising a new security threat to America itself. In early August, the UN Security Council unanimously passed new sanctions targeting North Korea's primary exports, with even Russia voting in favor this time (Roth 2017). Once North Korea threatened to strike Guam with its missiles, the president harshly countered with a guarantee of "fire and fury" if such aggression occurred (Vitali 2017). Administration officials, meanwhile, offered assurances that war with the rogue regime was not imminent.

Secretary of State Rex Tillerson in March indicated that years of diplomacy toward North Korea had failed to stem North Korean aggression and that it was time for the United States and its Asian allies to arrive at a new approach (Fifield and Gearan 2017). The options available to Trump when he took office, however, had not changed. The administration pursued increasing cooperation and engagement with China, Japan, and South Korea over the issue, along with development of antimissile capability and cyberwarfare activities against Kim Jong Un's regime. That approach may buy time but does not remove the underlying problem—the expansionist aggressiveness of North Korea.

The dire North Korean situation spurred Trump to curb for a while his long-standing criticism of China's trade practices. On April 16, he tweeted to his 28 million followers, "Why would I call China a currency manipulator when they are working with us on the North Korean problem? We will see what happens!" By the summer he was renewing trade threats against China, though, reflecting his frustration with their inability to improve the North Korea situation. China already had benefited from Trump's decision to withdraw from Obama's proposed Trans-Pacific Partnership trade agreement. The agreement sought to coordinate free trade agreements with eleven nations bordering the Pacific, including Canada, Mexico, Chile, and Japan—but not China. Its goal was to bring down taxes on exported goods among the nations, giving US consumers access to cheaper foreign goods but perhaps costing American jobs in the process. That cost had long inflamed Trump, who during the campaign had called it another "rape" by "special interests." He announced US withdrawal immediately after his inauguration (Popken 2017).

The Middle East and ISIS

No region of the globe has vexed more presidents than the Middle East. Barack Obama sought to downplay the US role in the region in favor of more engagement in Asian affairs. That did not work out so well. The result was a disastrous Syrian civil war that led to unprecedented numbers of refugees fleeing across the border to safe havens, many finding sanctuary in European nations and, in the process, roiling European politics.

The Middle East presented President Trump with at least seven major foreign policy problems. First, the Syrian civil war, with Russia and Iran supporting President Bashar al-Assad clinging to power while fighting a variety of insurgent forces, including the radical Islamist movement ISIS (Islamic

State in Iraq and Syria) and pro-Western rebels. Assad's forces have engaged in mass executions of his own citizens. Second, the challenge of ISIS, which seeks territorial expansion and exports terrorism while employing the most brutal methods. Third, Iran's development of nuclear weapons, supposedly delayed by a limitations agreement negotiated with Obama's diplomats but never submitted to the US Senate for treaty approval. Fourth, the role of ISIS and another Islamic fundamentalist movement, the Taliban, in the continuing insurgency against the Afghanistan government. The Taliban has sheltered and supported al-Qaeda, the organization responsible for the destruction of the World Trade Center on September 11, 2001. Fifth, in recent years US relations have deteriorated with Saudi Arabia and Egypt, both Sunni Islamic regimes deeply opposed to the Shia Islamic regime in Iran. Sixth, the long-standing territorial disputes between Israel and the adjoining Palestinian territories remained unresolved. Seventh, the collapse of Muammar Gaddafi's dictatorial regime in Libya produced disorder in which Islamic radicals gained presence and resources. A hornet's nest, indeed.

Candidate Trump offered pronouncements, many of them controversial, on the seven problems. On Syria, he renounced an earlier position in favor of accepting refugees and on the stump focused mainly on criticizing the Obama administration's policies. He uttered harsh rhetoric about ISIS, stating on August 2, 2016, "I would do what you have to do to get rid of ISIS. It's a horrific problem. . . . We have unleashed a monster in the Middle East. And, yes, I would bomb them—you have to do what you have to do to get rid of them" (Vladimirov 2016). The candidate indicated he would not publicize his plan in advance, letting his generals plan and execute it with the element of surprise.

Trump consistently denounced the Obama administration's nuclear treaty with Iran. In a speech before the American Israel Public Affairs Committee (AIPAC), he proclaimed, "My number one priority is to dismantle the disastrous deal with Iran. . . . We have rewarded the world's leading state sponsor of terror with $150 billion and we received absolutely nothing in return. . . . The biggest concern with the deal is not necessarily that Iran is going to violate it . . . the bigger problem is that they can keep the terms and still get to the bomb by simply running out the clock, and, of course, they keep the billions." Trump, in contrast, promised to "stand up" to Iran, dismantle its "global terror network," and hold Iran accountable for the negotiated agreement (Begley 2016).

Though in 2013 Trump proclaimed support of withdrawing US troops from Afghanistan, he changed his tune as a presidential candidate. Critical of a broad "nation-building" effort in the country, Trump indicated that, for purposes of national security, he would keep troops in the country. His goal now was defeat of the Taliban, though during the campaign he offered no specific plan to do so (Ramani 2016). Candidate Trump also made clear his support for Fattah el-Sisi, the autocratic ruler of Egypt whose human rights record had fallen into disfavor with the Obama White House. Trump voiced support for Egypt's cooperation in fighting terrorism. Trump met with el-Sisi at the United Nations on September 19. Also during the campaign, he had warned Saudi Arabia that he might cut off oil imports from that country if it did not enhance its efforts to combat Islamic terrorism.

Candidate Trump promised to be an ardent supporter of Israel. He met with Israel's prime minister, Binyamin Netanyahu, at Trump Tower in Manhattan on September 26, vowing to recognize Jerusalem as the capital of Israel, a move bitterly opposed by the Palestinian Authority (*Times of Israel* Staff 2016). In an earlier interview, the candidate voiced support for a "two-state solution" to the border problem as long as the Palestinian Authority recognized Israel's right to exist "as a Jewish state" (Sanger and Haberman 2016). Trump zigzagged about the overthrow of the Gaddafi regime in Libya. In February 2016 he disapproved of the removal of the Gaddafi regime in Libya, but by June he voiced approval for a "surgical strike" to remove the dictator. In his words: "I was never for strong intervention. I could have seen surgical where you take out Gadaffi and his group" (Cheney 2016).

Candidate Trump's views on the Middle East were a "work in progress" throughout 2016. Given his frequent alterations and qualifications of previous positions, it was far from clear how he would approach the region once in the White House. Would "America First" lead to more or less engagement with the troubled region? How dramatic would the policy changes be from those of the Obama administration? As Trump, once in office, learned more about the region and his options, Middle East policies did gradually emerge regarding the seven major challenges the region presented to him.

The Syrian civil war presented President Trump with a complex set of problems that obstructed development of a clear and constructive way forward for the United States. First, the myriad factions in the conflict—Assad and his Russian and Iranian sponsors, a collection of anti-Assad rebels including the Kurdish ethnic group, and the ISIS "caliphate" occupying considerable Syrian territory—made sorting through them a big challenge, as Obama had found in previous years. Obama's embrace of a nuclear deal with Iran made him unwilling to risk direct engagement with the pro-Iranian groups supporting President Assad. Trump had no such qualms, evident in his authorizing in early April a strike of 59 Tomahawk missiles on a pro-Assad military base in response to reports of the regime's use of chemical weapons on unarmed civilians. This humanitarian response received widespread praise.

Trump's broader Syrian policy, however, was tentative and populated by various voices not always in agreement. How could he work with Russia and Iran to defeat ISIS while also opposing the atrocity-prone Assad government? And what sort of government could ever bring peace to Syria? Secretary of Defense Mattis reportedly twice refused policy recommendations to broaden the anti-ISIS military offensive to take on pro-Iranian forces. This was proposed by National Security Council staff, but the Pentagon voiced no desire to directly combat pro-Assad forces (Brannan, De Luce, and McLeary 2017). The one imperative of the policy, often voiced by Trump, was the defeat of ISIS, to which he had allowed the Pentagon to devote additional military efforts beyond those permitted by Obama.

The battle against ISIS encountered complications because the United States backed anti-Assad rebels while Iran and Russian supported Assad, while all three nations fought against ISIS. The ground battle against ISIS enjoyed progress with the battle for Raqqa, the only major Syrian city still under ISIS control, commencing in early June. Attacking ISIS were Russian forces alongside a variety of Syrian Democratic rebel forces supported by the United States and its allies. Yet complications arose for the United States. A US warplane shot down an Iranian drone that had attacked US forces on patrol with allied Syrian rebels on June 8 as the battle for Raqqa commenced and on June 18 downed a Syrian government jet attacking US-backed rebels. Russia suspended cooperation with US air forces over parts of Syria as a result and threatened to attack any US planes hitting Assad's forces (Associated Press 2017a). Trump met with Putin in early July, resulting in an agreed ceasefire and "de-escalation zone" in southwest Iraq, auguring better cooperation between the nations in their fight against ISIS (Cohen and Liptak 2017).

The future of the civil war and Syria itself remains murky as the United States tries to defeat ISIS while also trying to find a way to remove Assad from power and install a better regime in his place. Trump has delegated military planning and tactics to his generals, but the diplomatic challenges for his administration remain great in this conflict. Can he continue to work with Russia effectively while it still props up the Assad regime that the United States opposes?

Trump, meanwhile, decided not to "tear up" the Iran nuclear deal as he had promised to do as a candidate. On May 17, his administration renewed the sanctions relief provided Iran under the accord and on July 17 reluctantly "recertified" Obama's Iran agreement. His administration had in recent months, however, announced new, narrower sanctions beyond those mentioned in the accord, placing sanctions on Iranians and Chinese companies and individuals supporting Iran's antiballistic missile program (De Luce 2017). The administration continued to label Iran as a leading "state sponsor of terrorism" and began a comprehensive review of its Iran policy.

Trump's tendency to delegate to his generals was again evident in the administration's Afghanistan policy. In June Secretary of Defense Mattis announced the additional deployment of a few thousand troops to the nation and promised an overall strategy by midsummer. He described his policymaking role as follows: "The president delegated the authority to me to turn the numbers up and down as necessary, but this came at the end of a very long discussion—months of discussion with the president as we looked at what the strategy is that would then guide how those numbers are decided. In other words I've been given some carte blanche to—to draw up a strategy or a number that's out of step with the strategy" (Gibbons-Neff and Lamothe 2017). By that point, the stalemate between the Afghan government and its Taliban-ISIS foes had been long standing. The long-term deployment seemed certain to continue under Trump, along with its steady stream of US casualties.

The president underscored his interest in improved relations with the Sunni Islamic government during a visit to Saudi Arabia in late May. This was part of the president's first extended foreign trip, which also took him to Israel, the Vatican, a NATO meeting in Brussels, and the G-7 summit of other industrial world powers in Italy. In Saudi Arabia, he met with Egyptian President el-Sisi and Saudi King Salman and promised to visit Egypt soon. President Trump announced a $110 billion sale of weapons to the Saudi monarchy and the opening there of a Global Center for Combating Extremist Ideology. He showered praise on Saudi Arabia, Egypt, Jordan, and the United Arab Emirates, all of which Trump views as allies in combating terrorism. In a public speech, he dramatically insisted, "A better future is only possible if your nations drive out the terrorists and extremists. Drive. Them. Out. DRIVE THEM OUT of your places of worship. DRIVE THEM OUT of your communities. DRIVE THEM OUT of your holy land, and DRIVE THEM OUT OF THIS EARTH" (CNN 2017). He was warmly received by the Saudi government, which had difficult relations with the Obama administration and strongly objected to Obama's Iranian nuclear accord.

Saudi Arabia, along with Egypt, Bahrain, and the United Arab Emirates, in early June announced a trade and diplomatic embargo of the Gulf nation of Qatar for its alleged support of Islamic extremism. The countries cut air, sea, and land links with Qatar. Several ordered Qataris in their countries to return home, and their citizens to leave the country within two weeks (Hennessey-Fiske 2017). President Trump tweeted his way into the controversy, first with this: "During my recent trip to the Middle East I stated that there can no longer be funding of Radical Ideology. Leaders pointed to Qatar - look!" Then a second tweet: "So good to see the Saudi Arabia visit with the King and 50 countries already paying off. They said they would take a hard line on funding . . . extremism, and all reference was pointing to Qatar. Perhaps this will be the beginning of the end to the horror of terrorism!" Senator Bob Corker (R-TN), when notified of the tweets by reporters, was unpleasantly surprised and responded, "It's been my policy that we work with all of our—we work with everybody in the region in a way that's constructive" (Kheel 2017).

Trump had complicated peace negotiations between Israel and the Palestinians in February by claiming the United States was no longer committed to the establishment of a Palestinian state on Israel's border—a big departure from previous US policy. In May, his visit to Israel included meeting with Israeli president Binyamin Netanyahu and Palestinian leader Mahmoud Abbas. During his stopover, he again declined to specifically advocate a two-state solution to the Israel-Palestinian border conflict. After returning to the United States, Trump delayed recognizing Jerusalem as the capital of Israel, which he had promised to do during the campaign. His wariness on both issues may have been a tactic to open up wide-ranging peace negotiations, which he enthusiastically seemed to support when in Israel (Gray 2017). His interest in negotiations was evident in June, when he sent son-in-law Jared Kushner to the region to facilitate Israeli-Palestinian peace talks in June.

The new president indicated far less interest in relations with factious post-Gaddafi Libya, declaring on April 21 that "I do not see a role in Libya. I think the United States has right now enough roles. We are in a role everywhere" (Kirchgaessner 2017). The president then indicated that he was concerned with Libya to the extent that it figured into efforts to combat ISIS. The United States at the time was on record as a strong supporter of the Tripoli government led by Fayez al-Sarraj. A rival government in eastern Libya, led by Khalifa Haftar, an anti-Islamist military strongman, had support from some parts of the Egyptian and Russian governments. US policy remained unclear in May as a leader of a rival Libyan faction traveled to Washington seeking support (Pecquet 2017).

Trump's early Middle East policies did not result in the dramatic changes he had proclaimed on the campaign stump. The Iranian peace deal was not "torn up," Jerusalem was not yet recognized as the capital of Israel, ISIS was not yet "destroyed," and only incremental change appeared in policies toward the US military involvement in Afghanistan and the Libyan situation. Certain presidential statements roiled the waters but did not yet seem tied to firm new policy directions—the Qatar tweets and disavowal of a two-state solution for the Israel-Palestinian dispute being examples of that. Initially, Trump in office was proving more cautious when handling the tinderbox region.

Europe

Probably no region of the world was more shaken by Trump's foreign policy direction than Europe, particularly the European Union (EU). The president managed to roil standing policies concerning the North Atlantic Treaty Organization (NATO), a decades-old mutual defense pact, and the Paris Climate Accord negotiated by President Obama. New arguments over transatlantic trade with European nations also erupted in the new Trump administration. Trump's initial immigration executive orders also received a cold reception from several European leaders.

A number of Trump's campaign positions were not welcomed by European officials. The candidate declared in a major foreign policy speech in late April, "In NATO, for instance, only 4 of 28 other member countries besides America, are spending the minimum required 2 percent of GDP on defense. . . . The countries we are defending must pay for the cost of this defense, and if not, the US must be prepared to let these countries defend themselves" (Diamond and Collinson 2016). He stated in early May that he supported the United Kingdom leaving the European Union, a diplomatic and economic coalition of which the nation had long been a member. In an interview in July 2016, the candidate indicated that he would not automatically come to the aid of Baltic nations if they encountered a Russian attack. Instead, he would first examine whether the nations had "fulfilled their obligations to us," probably through funding their militaries along NATO guidelines (Sanger and Haberman 2016). The candidate's opposition to the Trans-Pacific Partnership also augured poorly for the creation of a Transatlantic Trade and Investment Partnership (TIPP) with European nations. TIPP talks had been ongoing under Obama, but Trump's trade stance made their successful conclusion unlikely (Maher 2016).

When the Obama administration agreed to the Paris Climate Accord on October 5, 2016, Trump issued a statement labeling it a "bad deal" that would "impose enormous costs on American households through higher electricity prices and higher taxes" (Ballotpedia 2016). All European governments had signed the accord. Trump officially withdrew the United States from the accord on June 2. In the wake of his withdrawal, many state and local governments agreed to voluntary alliances to try to fulfill the goals of the Paris agreement.

Trump in office backtracked on his hostility to NATO. Though he declared it "obsolete" on January 17, by April 12 he admitted that he had made his January comment "not knowing much about NATO" and assuming it did little to fight terrorism. He had since learned otherwise: "They made a change and now they do fight terrorism. I said it was obsolete. It is no longer obsolete" (Mitchell 2017). But he stirred controversy during his late May visit to NATO headquarters by calling out most European nations for failing to maintain a NATO military contribution of 2 percent of GDP (gross domestic product) while refusing in his speech to reaffirm the United States' commitment to Article 5 of the NATO charter, which binds all member nations to join in the common defense of any nation under military attack. This very conspicuous omission surprised national security advisors and staff, who had expect Trump to verbally support Article 5 (Glasser 2017).

German chancellor Angela Merkel in response stated that Europe must "take its future into its own hands." The idea that Europe could depend on others—meaning the United States—was "over to a certain extent. This is what I have experienced in the last few days" (Farrell 2017). Trump fired back at Merkel in a tweet about trade on May 30: "We have a MASSIVE trade deficit with Germany, plus they pay FAR LESS than they should on NATO & military. Very bad for U.S. This will change." Trump eventually recanted his earlier NATO statement and in June gave verbal endorsement to the US obligations under Article 5 during a June press conference at the White House with the Romanian prime minister and later reaffirmed that commitment in a speech in Poland on the eve of July's G-20 summit (Associated Press 2017b).

Trump's provocative remarks and changing policy approaches contrasted with statements from his State and Defense Departments. Secretary of Defense Mattis, visiting Europe in February, consistently reassured European nations about the US commitment to NATO (Lamothe 2017). Secretary of State Tillerson looked forward to establishing environmental agreements with other nations in the wake of the rejection of the Paris climate treaty, a treaty he personally supported (Cama 2017). Whether these views would prevail with the president over time remained uncertain.

It became clear that "America First" to Trump does not involve the same sort of close diplomatic alignment with Europe that had characterized the Obama administration. Trump also has criticized the open immigration policies of Germany, Sweden, and other European nations, while touting the tighter immigration restrictions of eastern European nations like Hungary. Trump's approach to Europe suggests a more unilateral and much less multilateral orientation toward international relations. That unpredictability, he believes, is an asset for the United States internationally in that it keeps opponents guessing. It also makes Europe quite nervous about differences with his administration over common defense, climate change, immigration, and trade. That's no small list.

Russia

No aspect of Trump's foreign policy has attracted more media attention and public controversy than the president's relations with Russia. A widespread but unproven allegation holds that candidate Trump colluded with the Russian government in order to win the presidency. Trump himself fueled such suspicions through his offhand comments during his campaign and early months in the White House. The controversy, driven by a big wave of media coverage, has produced an investigation by Special Counsel Robert Mueller and inquiries by four congressional committees.

The Trump-Russia chronology reached back to December 2015, when retired Lieutenant General Mike Flynn, whom Trump would appoint as his national security advisor, received payment from the Russian government for participation in a panel discussion on the tenth anniversary for the Russia Today media operation. On March 28, 2016, veteran lobbyist Paul Manafort became Trump's campaign manager. In 2008, Manafort had lobbied for an ally of the Russian government and later assisted Russian-backed interests in Ukraine.

Then came the leaks. On June 15, 2016, a hacker calling himself "Guccifer 2.0" released the Democratic National Committee's research file on

Donald Trump. Russian hackers may have been the source of the leak. By July, the FBI had begun an investigation of possible links between the Trump campaign and Russian government. Trump foreign policy advisor Carter Page, with Trump campaign approval, delivered a lecture in Moscow. The FBI began secretly tracking Page's communications. Also in July, the Trump campaign got the Republican convention's platform committee to remove language calling for rearming Ukraine in response to Russian aggression. WikiLeaks on July 22 began leaking damaging emails stolen from the Democratic National Committee.

Trump then encouraged speculation about Russian involvement in his campaign by urging Russia to find 30,000 emails missing from Hillary Clinton's server. At a press conference in Florida, he proclaimed, "I will tell you this, Russia: If you're listening, I hope you find the 30,000 emails that are missing. I think you will probably be rewarded mightily by our press" (Crowley and Pager 2016). Following disclosures of possible secret Ukrainian payments to Paul Manafort, the Trump campaign fired him as its manager on August 19. Four days later, campaign advisor Roger Stone communicated with hacker Guccifer 2.0 privately over Twitter.

Congressional leaders in September received CIA briefings over the agency's belief that the Russian government was trying to help the Trump campaign. On October 7, the director of national intelligence and head of the Department of Homeland Security released a public statement warning of possible Russian interference in the election and involvement in the WikiLeaks disclosures.

In the wake of the election, President Obama warned Trump against hiring General Michael Flynn. Obama had fired Flynn in 2014 as head of the Defense Intelligence Agency because of his disruptive leadership style (Miller and Goldman 2014). Appointed as national security advisor on November 18, Flynn was told by the Trump transition team that his communications with Russian ambassador Sergei Kislyak, with whom he had been in contact in recent months, would henceforth be monitored by US intelligence agencies. In early December, Flynn and Trump son-in-law Jared Kushner met with Kislyak at Trump Tower, and Flynn had repeated conversations with the Russian ambassador in December. Obama placed additional sanctions on Russia in response to reports of their interference in the 2016 US elections. Trump then lauded Putin for not replying in kind to Obama's sanctions.

After Trump's inauguration, the FBI interviewed Flynn about his December conversations with Kislyak. Flynn then got himself in trouble by contradicting public statements by Vice President Pence regarding an FBI interview concerning Russia. The contradiction caused the White House to lose confidence in him, and he was forced to resign on February 13. Meanwhile, former senator (R-AL) and new attorney general Jefferson Sessions found himself involved in a controversy over his public statements about meetings with Russian officials in 2016. Sessions explained that two meetings with Kislyak occurred during his duties as a member of the Foreign Relations Committee and not as an emissary of the Trump campaign.

Trump on February 14 met with FBI director James Comey, who had confirmed that an FBI investigation of Russian hacking and possible links to the Trump campaign was underway. In the meeting, Trump, according to Comey, called Flynn a "good guy" and hoped Comey, regarding an investigation of Flynn, could "let this go." Sessions recused himself from any role in the FBI investigation because of reports of his 2016 meetings with Russians. As the FBI and congressional investigations proceeded, Trump abruptly fired Comey on May 9, calling the Russia probe a "made-up story," and then raised suspicions by conducting a meeting with Russian foreign minister Sergey Lavrov and Kislyak the next day. On May 17, Deputy Attorney General Rod Rosenstein appointed former FBI director Robert Mueller to examine the Russian role in the Trump administration and 2016 elections (Bump 2017). Evidence then emerged of a meeting between Donald Trump Jr. and several Russians in June 2016. Trump acquaintance and music promoter Bob Goldstone promised damaging information regarding Hillary Clinton if he would meet with Russian lawyer Natalia Veselnitskaya. Trump Jr. responded in an email, "If that's what you say, I love it." Campaign director Paul Manafort, Jared Kushner, and Trump Jr. attended a June 9 meeting with Veselnitskaya and three other Russians. Trump Jr., when releasing his emails about the meeting, described it as brief and unproductive and primarily concerned with changing US policy toward Russian adoptions. All of those at the meeting were likely to appear before congressional and Robert Mueller's investigators (Kinery 2017). Kushner in his July congressional testimony asserted, "I did not collude, and did not know anyone else in the campaign who colluded, with any foreign government" (Kushner 2017).

There is much suggestive smoke in the above narrative, but no firm evidence of fire. Russia has a long history of attempted involvement in US elections (Walton 2016), and communications between the Russian government and an incoming administration is a routine part of transition business. Trump raised eyebrows with his campaign references to Russia's election involvement and his firing of FBI Director Comey. Michael Flynn quickly destroyed his credibility as national security advisor, and Paul Manafort's Ukrainian ties remain under investigation. Yet Manafort lost his job in August, and Flynn was quickly sacked in February.

Donald Jr.'s aspirations for campaign "dirt" on Hillary Clinton prompted his meeting with Russians, but so far there is no clear evidence that such "dirt" was discussed or delivered during the meeting. Beyond these serious concerns, no indisputable evidence of sustained and successful campaign collusion with Russia has been established despite months of ongoing investigations. Trump, however, created the media specter of possible obstruction of justice in his sacking of Comey, even though the president has full legal authority to remove the director.

Russia has dominated media headlines about the new administration due to the ongoing FBI and congressional investigations. Trump himself has created political problems regarding the matter with his constant stream of tweets about the "fake" Russia story, in effect helping to keep alive a controversy damaging to his presidency. It's a curious case of self-destructive presidential behavior.

How has policy toward Russia shifted in the early Trump presidency? The administration has coordinated a more aggressive military response to ISIS with Russia. Yet the White House has also directed bombing against Syrian President Assad, a Russian client, in response to evidence of humanitarian atrocities by Assad's regime. Congress overwhelmingly passed enhanced sanctions on Russia, which the president signed (Lardner 2017). Trump met with President Putin twice during the G-20 meetings in early July. The two agreed on clear military borders for their Syria operations, but no further signs of enhanced cooperation emerged. In short, no major redirection in Russian policy has yet appeared despite the president's repeated statements of willingness to work with Putin on issues of mutual interest.

Trump did, however, institute partial policy change toward the former Russian client state of Cuba. He reversed aspects of Obama's diplomatic and commercial opening to Cuba. Trump kept the US embassy open but placed new travel and commercial restrictions on Cuba. He prohibited commerce with companies owned by Cuban intelligence services and the military and more strictly enforced the granting of travel exemptions to the island, making it much harder for US citizens to visit the island. Trump asserted he would "expose the crimes of the Castro regime" (Merica 2017). Trump's action came despite an interagency review by the State Department that recommended keeping the policy in place. Trump's new approach would not "have a nuclear impact to Obama's policies," according to one former State Department official, "but it will add a lot of uncertainty to an already uncertain environment" (Gramer 2017).

THE REALISTS: TRUMP AND OBAMA

It may seem strange to conclude by noting how Obama and Trump share a common perspective on foreign policy. Trump's nationalistic and brash style contrasts with Obama's more cerebral and temperate approach to foreign affairs. Yet both can be labeled as "realists" in their approach to foreign policy.

Realism is rooted in several assumptions. First, the international order is made up of nation-states, each concerned with its own power and security. Military and economic power are the prime guarantors of national security. A stable international order results from a stable balance of power between nation-states. Realism is best understood in its contrast with the rival approach of liberalism, which argues that ever more complex ties between nations have made it increasingly difficult to define national interest and have decreased the usefulness of military power. Foreign policy liberals seek to build strong multilateral institutions, such as the United Nations and European Union, in order to lessen the primacy of the nation-state in international affairs and, correspondingly, to reduce the use of military force. International human rights and international law are much more important goals to liberals than to realists (*Stanford Encyclopedia* 2017).

Trump is an exuberant realist who thinks of the world in terms of America's national interest. "America First" means employing the nation's economic and military power to improve the life of its citizens. Other nations are useful to the extent that they contribute to Trump's primarily national goals. Trump's tools include employing negotiation and unpredictability in pursuing national ends. Former Obama Defense Department appointee Rosa Brooks summarizes Trump's view:

> Trump has little . . . time for multilateralist diplomats: they're too willing to compromise, trading away American interests in exchange for platitudes about friendship and cooperation. And he has no time at all for those who consider long-standing U.S. alliances sacrosanct. To Trump, U.S. alliances, like potential business partners in a real-estate transaction, should always be asked: "What have you done for me lately?" In his inimitable way, Trump is offering a powerful challenge to many of the core assumptions of Washington's bipartisan foreign-policy elite. (Brooks 2016)

Trump believes Obama failed at protecting the nation's interests—"total failure" is how he described his predecessor's foreign policy in a tweet. Obama's trade policy failed to stop the export of jobs overseas, with the Trans-Pacific Partnership an example of that misguided approach. He has tolerated unacceptable trade practices by China. His attempt to disengage from the Middle East led to a disastrous civil war in Syria and the rise of the ISIS caliphate, a new and dangerous threat to America's national security. Obama's Iran nuclear deal boosts the power of a main sponsor of international terrorism and won't stop that nation from eventually gaining nuclear weapons. His North Korea policy was ineffectual. And so on.

Given this criticism, how can Obama also be termed a foreign policy realist? He admittedly differed from Trump in his choice of both strategy and tactics toward the globe. Barack Obama, however, professed an admiration for the foreign policy of George H. W. Bush and his national security advisor, Brent Skowcroft, in office from 1989 to 1993. Their foreign policy was realist, but with a greater emphasis on predictability, diplomacy, and multilateral cooperation than Trump has thus far pursued. This Obama statement contradicts Trump's now evident tactics: "I think that the best argument you can make on the side of those who are critics of my foreign policy is that the president doesn't exploit ambiguity enough. He doesn't maybe react in ways that might cause people to think, *Wow, this guy might be a little crazy*" (Goldberg 2016).

Obama's realist approach is reflected in many of his strategies, including "deal with the world as it is, not as we wish it were . . . adapt to differences in different situations . . . pay heed to geopolitics . . . states have no permanent friends or allies, only permanent interests" (Pillar 2016). These are approaches evident in Trump's view of the world as well. Both believe that the world is a collection of nation-states each primarily concerned with its own interests and often in competition with each other.

It's easy to overstate the foreign policy differences between the two realist presidents. After six months in office, Trump's actual shifts from the previous administration's foreign policies are less than comprehensive in scope. A *Washington Post* policy survey at the end of Trump's first six months in office found that he had altered greatly Obama's foreign policies in only four areas: the Trans-Pacific Partnership, the Syrian war, the travel ban, and Paris Climate Accord. Limited or no change had occurred in eleven foreign policy areas: Russia, North Korea, the ISIS war, NATO, the North American Free Trade Agreement, China, Afghanistan, the Mexican border wall, Cuba, the Iran nuclear deal, and the Israel-Palestinian conflict (Fischer-Baum and Vitkovskaya 2017).

What distinguishes Trump from Obama, however, is his differing empirical assessment of America's status in the world. Obama saw climate change, Russian aggression, and a growing Asia as immediate national concerns. For Trump, the United States faces trade disasters, nations that need to pay more for their own defense, and the strong threat of international terrorism.

Obama believed in cautious pursuit of national interest through diplomacy and multilateral agreements, when possible. Trump is more prone to rely on military and commercial power in pursuit of those interests. That produced a Trump foreign policy diverging from that of Obama. The divergence stems from Trump's different view of the threats facing America and contrasting choice of strategies and tactics to address those threats. The presidents are two realists with dissimilar conceptions of America's national interests and how to pursue them.

WORKS CITED

Almasy, Steve, and Darran Simon. "A Timeline of President Trump's Travel Bans." CNN. March 30, 2017. http://www.cnn.com/2017/02/10/us/trump-travel-ban-timeline/index.html (accessed June 16, 2017).

Associated Press. "The Latest: Russian Threatens after US Downs Syrian Airplane." June 20, 2017a. https://apnews.com/35ea1dae18c94c52ac8bf54e1c5fa8a5/The-Latest:-Russia-warns-US-after-downing-of-Syrian-jet (accessed June 22, 2017).

Associated Press. "President Trump Confirms His Commitment to NATO's Article 5 Mutual Defense Pact." *Time*. June 9, 2017b. http://time.com/4813299/donald-trump-nato-article-5/ (accessed June 22, 2017).

Ballotpedia.org. "Donald Trump Campaign, 2016/Foreign Affairs." November 8, 2016. https://ballotpedia.org/Donald_Trump_presidential_campaign,_2016/Foreign_affairs (accessed June 22, 2017).

Beckwith, Ryan Teague. "Read Donald Trump's 'America First' Foreign Policy Speech." *Time*. April 27, 2016. http://time.com/4309786/read-donald-trumps-america-first-foreign-policy-speech/?xid=time_socialflow_twitter (accessed June 16, 2017).

Begley, Sarah. "Read Donald Trump's Speech to AIPAC." *Time*. March 21, 2016. http://time.com/4267058/donald-trump-aipac-speech-transcript/ (accessed June 17, 2017).

Bennett, John T. "Trump's First Memos Set Up Conflict with GOP." *Roll Call*. January 23, 2017. http://www.rollcall.com/news/politics/trumps-first-memos-sets-conflict-gop (accessed June 16, 2017).

Berenson, Tessa. "How Donald Trump Flip-Flopped on 3 Major Issues." *Time*. March 7, 2016. http://time.com/4249568/donald-trump-flip-flops-issues/ (accessed June 16, 2017).

Brannan, Kate, Dan De Luce, and Paul McLeary. "Mattis Overrules White House Radicals on Syria Policy." *Newsweek*. June 19, 2017. http://www.newsweek .com/mattis-overrules-white-house-radicals-syria-policy-627248 (accessed June 22, 2017).

Brooks, Rosa. "Donald Trump Has a Coherent, Realist Foreign Policy." *Foreign Policy*. April 12, 2016. http://foreignpolicy.com/2016/04/12/donald-trump-has -a-coherent-realist-foreign-policy/ (accessed June 29, 2017).

Bump, Philip. "Timeline: What We Know about Trump's Campaign, Russia and the Investigation of the Two." June 6, 2017. https://www.washingtonpost.com/ news/politics/wp/2017/05/30/timeline-what-we-know-about-trumps-campaign -russia-and-the-investigation-of-the-two/?utm_term=.64bd1f72c6d1 (accessed June 29, 2017).

Cama, Timothy. "Tillerson: 'My View Didn't Change' on Paris Climate Agreement." *The Hill*. June 13, 2017. http://thehill.com/policy/energy-environment /337578-tillerson-my-view-didnt-change-on-paris-climate-agreement (accessed June 22, 2017).

CBS News. "Trump on Assassinating Kim Jong Un: 'I've Heard of Worse Things.'" February 10, 2016. http://www.cbsnews.com/news/donald-trump -assassinating-north-korean-leader-kim-jong-un-china-role/ (accessed June 17, 2017).

Cheney, Kyle. "Trump Shifts Position on Libya." *Politico*. June 5, 2016. http:// www.politico.com/story/2016/06/libya-donald-trump-qadhafi-223911 (accessed June 17, 2017).

CNN. "Transcript of Trump's Speech in Saudi Arabia." May 21, 2017. http://www .cnn.com/2017/05/21/politics/trump-saudi sphttp://www.cnn.com/2017/05/21/ politics/trump-saudi-speech-transcript/index.htmleech-transcript/index.html (accessed June 22, 2017).

Cohen, Zachary, and Aaron Liptak. "Tillerson: Trump, Putin Reach Ceasefire Agreement." CNN. July 8, 2017. http://www.cnn.com/2017/07/07/politics/ syria-ceasefire-us-russia-tillerson/index.html (accessed July 25, 2017).

Crowley, Michael, and Tyler Pager. 2016. "Trump Urges Russia to Hack Clinton's email." *Politico*. http://www.politico.com/story/2016/07/trump-putin-no -relationship-226282 (accessed June 29, 2017).

De Luce, Dan. "Trump Keeps the Iran Deal Alive, For Now." *Foreign Policy*. May 17, 2017. http://foreignpolicy.com/2017/05/17/trump-keeps-the-iran-deal-alive -for-now/ (accessed June 22, 2017).

de Vogue, Ariane. "Supreme Court Says Grandparents, Relatives Can Enter US Despite Travel Ban." CNN. July 19, 2017. http://www.cnn.com/2017/07/

19/politics/supreme-court-travel-ban-grandparents/index.html (accessed July 25, 2017).

Diamond, Jeremy, and Stephen Collinson. "Donald Trump's Foreign Policy: 'America First.'" CNN. April 27, 2016. http://www.cnn.com/2016/04/27/politics/donald-trump-foreign-policy-speech/index.html (accessed June 22, 2017).

Farrell, Henry. "Thanks to Trump, Germany Says It Can't Rely on the United States. What Does That Mean?" *Washington Post*. May 28, 2017. https://www.washingtonpost.com/news/monkey-cage/wp/2017/05/28/thanks-to-trump-germany-says-it-cant-rely-on-america-what-does-that-mean/?utm_term=.c3494beefe1a (accessed June 22, 2017).

Fifield, Anna, and Anne Gearan. "Tillerson Says Diplomacy with North Korea Has 'Failed'; Pyongyang Warns of War." *Washington Post*. March 16, 2017. https://www.washingtonpost.com/world/asia_pacific/tillerson-stresses-regional-cooperation-to-curb-north-koreas-weapons-programs/2017/03/16/4ec5e07c-09ab-11e7-bd19-fd3afa0f7e2a_story.html?utm_term=.f7b33de07faa (accessed June 17, 2017).

Fischer-Baum, Reuben, and Julie Vitkovskaya. "How Trump Is Changing America's Foreign Policy." *Washington Post*. July 25, 2017. https://www.washingtonpost.com/graphics/2017/world/trump-shifting-alliances/?utm_term=.c390a0730eeb (accessed July 25, 2017).

Gibbons-Neff, Thomas, and Dan Lamothe. "'What's Your Endgame?' Trump Delegating Afghan War Decisions to the Pentagon Faces Scrutiny." *Washington Post*. June 14, 2017. https://www.washingtonpost.com/news/checkpoint/wp/2017/06/14/whats-your-end-game-trump-delegating-afghan-war-decisions-to-the-pentagon-faces-scrutiny/?utm_term=.1b4b8b99 (accessed June 22, 2017).

Glasser, Susan B. "Trump National Security Team Blindsided by NATO Speech." *Politico*. June 5, 2017. http://www.politico.com/magazine/story/2017/06/05/trump-nato-speech-national-security-team-215227 (accessed June 22, 2017).

Goldberg, Jeffrey. "The Obama Doctrine." *The Atlantic*. April 2016. https://www.theatlantic.com/magazine/archive/2016/04/the-obama-doctrine/471525/ (accessed June 29, 2017).

Gramer, Robbie. "Trump Snubs State, Will Partially Reverse Obama's Cuba Policy." *Foreign Policy*. June 16, 2017. http://foreignpolicy.com/2017/06/16/trump-snubs-state-will-partially-reverse-obamas-cuba-policy/ (accessed June 29, 2017).

Gray, Rosie. "Trump Leaves Israel Pushing Peace, but Staying Vague." *The Atlantic*. May 23, 2017. https://www.theatlantic.com/international/archive/2017/05/trump-israeli-palestinian-peace/527739/ (accessed June 22, 2017).

Hennessey-Fiske, Molly. "Tiny Qatar Refuses to Bend on Foreign Policy despite a Blockade by Other Persian Gulf Nations." *Los Angeles Times*. June 16, 2017. http://www.latimes.com/world/middleeast/la-fg-qatar-explainer-2017-story.html (accessed June 22, 2017).

Hensch, Mark. "Clinton Camp: Trump's Immigration Address His 'Darkest Speech.'" *The Hill*. September 1, 2016. http://thehill.com/blogs/ballot-box/ presidential-races/294059-clinton-camp-trumps-immigration-talk-his-darkest -speech (accessed June 16, 2017).

Jarrett, Laura, and Ariane de Vogue. "9th Circuit Deals Trump's Travel Ban Another Defeat." CNN. June 13, 2017. http://www.cnn.com/2017/06/12/ politics/9th-circuit-travel-ban/index.html (accessed June 16, 2017).

Kheel, Rebecca. "Foreign Relations Chair Stunned by Trump's Qatar Tweets." *The Hill*. June 6, 2017. http://thehill.com/policy/defense/336557-foreign -relations-chairman-stunned-silenced-by-trumps-qatar-tweets (accessed June 22, 2017).

Kinery, Emma. "Timeline: Donald Trump Jr.'s Interactions with Kremlin-Linked Lawyer." *USA Today*. July 11, 2017. https://www.usatoday.com/story/ news/politics/2017/07/11/timeline-donald-trump-jr-interactions-kremlin-linked -lawyer/467634001/ (accessed July 23, 2017).

Kirchgaessner, Stephanie. "Donald Trump Remarks Raise Fears of US Disengage-ment from Libya." *Guardian*. April 21, 2017. https://www.theguardian.com/ world/2017/apr/21/donald-trump-remarks-raise-fears-of-us-disengagement-in -libya (accessed June 22, 2017).

Kopan, Tal. "Trump Seeks $1.6 Billion for 'Border Wall' Bricks and Mortar." CNN. May 23, 2017. http://www.cnn.com/2017/05/23/politics/trump-budget -border-security/index.html (accessed June 16, 2017).

Kushner, Jared. "Statement of Jared C. Kushner to Congressional Committees." July 24, 2017. https://www.documentcloud.org/documents/3899497-Jared-Kushner -July-24-Statement-to-Congressional.html?utm_campaign=SocialFlow&utm_ source=Twitter&utm_medium=AP (accessed July 24, 2017).

Lamothe, Dan. "Mattis Attempts to Reassure NATO Allies as the Trump Adminis-tration Deals with Fallout from Flynn's Ouster." *Washington Post*. February 15, 2017. https://www.washingtonpost.com/news/checkpoint/wp/2017/02/15/mattis -attempts-to-reassure-nato-allies-as-the-trump-administration-deals-with-fall out-from-flynns-ouster/?utm_term=.ecbb8ab68cac (accessed June 22, 2017).

Lardner, Richard. "The White House Says Trump Will Sign a New Russia Sanc-tions Bill." *Time*. July 23, 2017. http://time.com/4870392/trump-sign-russia -sanctions-bill/ (accessed July 25, 2017).

Lee, Michelle Ye Hee. "Fact Checker: President Trump's Claim That Illegal Im-migration Is Down 64 Percent Because of His Administration." *Washington Post*. April 11, 2017. https://www.washingtonpost.com/news/fact-checker/ wp/2017/04/11/president-trumps-claim-that-illegal-immigration-is-down-64 -percent-because-of-his-administration/?utm_term=.0cd61cbb2fec (accessed June 16, 2017).

Lu, Sheng. "Timeline of Trade Policy in the Trump Administration." University of Delaware. Department of Fashion and Apparel Studies. May 18, 2017. https://shenglufashion.wordpress.com/timeline-of-trade-policy-in-the-trump-administration/ (accessed June 16, 2017).

Maher, Richard. "3 Reasons European Leaders Oppose Trump." *US News and World Report.* November 3, 2016. https://www.usnews.com/news/best-countries/articles/2016-11-03/3-reasons-why-european-leaders-oppose-donald-trump (accessed June 22, 2017).

McGraw, Meridith, and Adam Kelsey. "A Timeline of Trump's Immigration Executive Order and Legal Challenges." ABC News. March 16, 2017. http://abcnews.go.com/Politics/timeline-president-trumps-immigration-executive-order-legal-challenges/story?id=45332741 (accessed June 16, 2017).

McKirdy, Euan. "North Korea Timeline: From Trump's Inauguration to Now." CNN. June 8, 2017. http://www.cnn.com/2017/04/18/asia/north-korea-donald-trump-timeline/index.html (accessed June 17, 2017).

Merica, Dan. "Trump Unveils New Restrictions on Travel, Business in Cuba." CNN. June 17, 2017. http://www.cnn.com/2017/06/16/politics/trump-cuba-policy/index.html (accessed June 29, 2017).

Miller, Greg, and Adam Goldman. "Head of Pentagon Intelligence Agency Forced Out, Officials Say." *Washington Post.* April 30, 2014. https://www.washingtonpost.com/world/national-security/head-of-pentagon-intelligence-agency-forced-out-officials-say/2014/04/30/ec15a366-d09d-11e3-9e25-188ebe1fa93b_story.html?utm_term=.9d5c587751c7 (accessed June 29, 2017).

Mitchell, Ellen. "Trump Didn't Know 'Much' about NATO When He Called It Obsolete: Report." *The Hill.* April 24, 2017. http://thehill.com/policy/international/330245-trump-didnt-know-much-about-nato-when-he-called-it-obsolete-report (accessed June 22, 2017).

Murphy, John G. "What Trade Really Means for Pennsylvania and Ohio." US Chamber of Commerce. June 28, 2016. https://www.uschamber.com/above-the-fold/what-trade-really-means-pennsylvania-and-ohio?utm_content=sf29843486&utm_medium=spredfast&utm_source=twitter&utm_campaign=U.S.+Chamber+of+Commerce&sf29843486=1 (accessed June 16, 2017).

Murphy, Mike. "Trump: China Not a Currency Manipulator; Trade Deficit OK in Exchange for Help on North Korea." *MarketWatch.* April 12, 2017. http://www.marketwatch.com/story/trump-china-not-a-currency-manipulator-trade-deficit-ok-in-exchange-for-help-on-north-korea-2017-04-12 (accessed June 16, 2017).

Nakamura, David. "Trump Administration Issues New Immigration Enforcement Policies, Says Goal Is Not "Mass Deportations."" *Washington Post.* February 21, 2017. https://www.washingtonpost.com/politics/trump-administration-seeks-to-prevent-panic-over-new-immigration-enforcement-policies/2017/02/21/a2a695a8-f847-11e6-bf01-d47f8cf9b643_story.html?utm_term=.c800215a0113 (accessed June 16, 2017).

Neuhauser, Alan. "6 Differences Between the New and Old Travel Bans." *US News and World Report*. March 6, 2017. https://www.usnews.com/news/national-news/articles/2017-03-06/6-differences-between-trumps-new-and-old-travel-bans (accessed June 16, 2017).

Osborne, Samuel. *Independent*. "Donald Trump Admits Xi Jinping Gave Him a History Lesson on North Korea." April 13, 2017. http://www.independent.co.uk/news/world/americas/us-politics/donald-trump-xi-jingping-north-korea-history-lesson-10-minute-china-us-talks-mar-a-lago-florida-a7681611.html (accessed June 17, 2017).

Pecquet, Julian. "Libyan Rivals Descend on Washington." *Al-Monitor*. May 8, 2017. http://www.al-monitor.com/pulse/originals/2017/05/libya-rivals-washington-trump-hifter-sarraj.html (accessed June 22, 2017).

Pillar, Paul R. "Obama the Realist." *The National Interest*. March 12, 2016. http://nationalinterest.org/blog/paul-pillar/obama-the-real http://nationalinterest.org/blog/paul-pillar/obama-the-realist-15479?page=showist-15479?page=show (accessed June 29, 2017).

Popken, Ben. "Why Trump Killed The TPP—And Why It Matters To You." NBC News. January 23, 2017. http://www.nbcnews.com/business/economy/why-trump-killed-tpp-why-it-matters-you-n710781 (accessed June 17, 2017).

Ramani, Samuel. "What a Trump Presidency Would Mean for Afghanistan." *The Diplomat*. August 2, 2016. http://thediplomat.com/2016/08/what-a-trump-presidency-would-mean-for-afghanistan/ (accessed June 17, 2017).

Roth, Richard. "UN Security Council Imposes New Sanctions on North Korea." CNN. August 6, 2017. http://www.cnn.com/2017/08/05/asia/north-korea-un-sanctions/index.html (accessed August 14, 2017).

Sanger, David, and William J. Broad. "Trump Inherits a Secret Cyberwar Against North Korean Missiles." *New York Times*. March 4, 2017. https://www.nytimes.com/2017/03/04/world/asia/north-korea-missile-program-sabotage.html?_r=0 (accessed June 17, 2017).

Sanger, David, and Maggie Haberman. "Highlights from Our Interview with Donald Trump on Foreign Policy." *New York Times*. March 26, 2016. https://www.nytimes.com/2016/03/27/us/.../donald-trump-interview-highlights.html (accessed June 17, 2017).

Stanford Encyclopedia of Philosophy. 2017. "Political Realism in International Relations." https://plato.stanford.edu/entries/realism-intl-relations/ (accessed June 29, 2017).

Stern, Mark Joseph. "Fourth Circuit Upholds Travel Ban Injunction, Saying It Drips with 'Religious Intolerance.'" *Slate*. May 25, 2017a. http://www.slate.com/blogs/the_slatest/2017/05/25/fourth_circuit_upholds_injunction_on_trump_s_travel_ban.html (accessed June 16, 2017).

Stern, Mark Joseph. "The 9th Circuit Just Gave the Supreme Court a New Tool to Block Trump's Travel Ban." *Slate*. June 12, 2017b. http://www.slate.com/

blogs/the_slatest/2017/06/12/ninth_circuit_maintains_injunction_against_
trump_s_travel_ban.html (accessed June 16, 2017).

Team Fix. "Transcript of the New Hampshire GOP Debate, Annotated." *Washington Post*. February 6, 2016. https://www.washingtonpost.com/news/the
-fix/wp/2016/02/06/transcript-of-the-feb-6-gop-debate-annotated/?utm_term=
.a57395e78f1b (accessed June 17, 2017).

Time Staff. "Read Donald Trump's Speech on Trade." *Time*. June 28, 2016. http://
time.com/4386335/donald-trump-trade-speech-transcript/ (accessed June 16,
2017).

Times of Israel Staff. "Trump to Netanyahu: If I'm President, I'll Recognize Undivided Jerusalem." *Times of Israel*. September 25, 2016. http://www.timesof
israel.com/pm-meets-trump-in-ny-will-sit-down-with-clinton-later/ (accessed
June 17, 2017).

Timm, Jane C. "Tracking President Trump's Flip-Flops." NBC News. May 12,
2017. http://www.nbcnews.com/storyline/president-trumps-first-100-days/here
-are-new-policy-stances-donald-trump-has-taken-election-n684946 (accessed
June 16, 2017).

Vitali, Ali. "Trump on North Korea Feud: 'Fire and Fury' not Tough Enough."
NBC News. August 10, 2017. http://www.nbcnews.com/politics/white-house/
trump-north-korea-feud-fire-fury-not-tough-enough-n791561 (accessed August
14, 2017).

Vladimirov, Nikita. "Trump: US Has 'No Choice But to Bomb' ISIS in Libya."
The Hill. August 2, 2016. http://thehill.com/blogs/ballot-box/presidential-races/
290115-trump-us-has-no-choice-but-to-bomb-isis-in-libya?utm_source=&utm_
medium=email&utm_campaign=3317 (accessed June 17, 2017).

Walton, Calder. "'Active Measures': A History of Russian Interference in US
Elections." *Prospect*. December 23, 2016. http://www.prospectmagazine.co.uk/
science-and-technology/active-measures-a-history-of-russian-interference-in
-us-elections (accessed June 29, 2017).

White House. Office of the Press Secretary. "Executive Order Protecting the
Nation from Foreign Terrorist Entry into the United States." March 6, 2017.
https://www.whitehouse.gov/the-press-office/2017/03/06/executive-order-pro
tecting-nation-foreign-terrorist-entry-united-states (accessed June 16, 2017).

6

Trump's Prospects

@realDonaldTrump
The era of division is coming to an end. We will create a new future of #AmericanUnity. First, we need to #DrainTheSwamp!
(9:47 p.m., October 19, 2016)

As much as he may desire it, Donald Trump's desire to preside over a new era of American unity has not come to pass and is unlikely to arrive during his time in the White House. Trump's tweets, showcasing his penchant for unproductive verbal conflict, are part of the reason why national unity will not arrive soon. But the reasons for national division and contentiousness extend far beyond Trump himself. Over the last thirty years, US politics has grown increasingly more polarized between Democrats and Republicans. Two aspects characterize the polarization. First, those who are politically active "divide strongly on many major issues before the country." Second, within the two parties their activists "hold relatively uniform issue positions" (Schier and Eberly 2016, 6). Trump's querulous persona just adds fuel to this fire.

To the picture of Trump and polarization we must add three traits of the current political environment determining Trump's future prospects as president. First, economic conditions—particularly rising inequality and the loss of US manufacturing jobs to foreign competitors—helped to shape a growing popular discontent with politics as usual. The discontent encompasses low trust that government will do "what is right" and a widespread belief that it cares little for the concerns of ordinary citizens (Schier and Eberly 2013, 29). A result is a political era of "partisan volatility" in which governing alignments are unstable. Trump's rise is both a symptom and a product of that volatility. That volatility is also a major impediment to his future governing and electoral success.

DEFINING TRAITS OF CONTEMPORARY US POLITICS

Rising economic inequality and the loss of many high-quality US manufacturing jobs have roiled US politics in recent decades and helped propel Donald Trump into the White House. The US Census Bureau has charted a steady rise in income inequality since 1993.

By 2014, "the top 5% of households received 21.8% of 'equivalence-adjusted' aggregate income, while the bottom 60% received just 27.1%. Equivalence-adjusted estimates factor in different household sizes and compositions" (Desilver 2015). Despite a 5.2 percent increase in middle-class incomes in 2015, income inequality remained stable (Luhby 2016). Wealth differences have grown even more pronounced. A Pew Center report found that in 2013, the median net worth of the nation's upper-income families was 6.6 times that of middle-income families, and nearly 70 times that of lower-income families. The analysis also found that since 1983, virtually all of the wealth gains made by US families have gone to the upper-income group (Fry and Kochhar 2014).

Lots of Americans feel they are economically falling behind as time passes. The nation's middle class has suffered from income stagnation and rising personal debt in recent decades. Aggregate incomes in 2015 remained 1.6 percent lower than in 2000 and 2.4 percent below their 1999 peak. Median earnings for men working full-time remained lower than they were in the 1970s (Luhby 2016). The Federal Reserve reported in 2013 that the average debt of middle-class families—those that fall within the middle three-fifths of the population by earnings—amounted to an estimated 122 percent of annual income, nearly double the level of 1989 (Federal Reserve 2013).

The stagnation of male income reflects the big loss of US manufacturing since their peak in 1979. The Bureau of Labor Statistics reported that by 2015, 7,231,000 such jobs had disappeared since 1979, a 37 percent decline (Bureau of Labor Statistics 2017). The rise of automation and strong foreign competition spawned this decline.

Edward Alden, senior fellow at the Council of Foreign Relations, summarizes the import of all these statistical trends. "The United States has faced increased import competition in a growing number of economic sectors that once employed millions of people at generally higher wages than they could earn at other jobs. . . . Those who lose their jobs to computers are likely to find new ones, while those who lose their jobs to imports are much less likely to do so" (Alden 2017, 5). The implications for many middle-class Americans are ominous: "But far too many Americans are simply unprepared for the competition they are now in. They are like overmatched boxers who keep getting knocked down, only to be told by their corner that they just have to get back in the ring and keep taking the punches in the hope that eventually they will become better fighters" (Alden 2017, 17). It is precisely this discontent that candidate Trump exploited with his assaults on foreign trade and assertion that "America doesn't win anymore."

Americans' political attitudes altered as these economic trends persisted. Alongside Americans' income and debt difficulties came widespread and growing popular discontent with government, a trend that began in the late 1960s and persisted through the 2016 election. The immediate causes of the discontent were divisive events of the sixties and seventies: Vietnam, the Civil Rights revolution, and Watergate along with the persistent economic problems of the 1970s (Nye and Zelikow 1997). University of Michigan surveys since 1960 have asked four questions about trust in government—a "trust index" and also a question about popular discontent, querying whether government officials "care much about what people like me think." The measures vary inversely—lower trust and higher discontent—in a strong pattern since 1964 (Schier and Eberly 2013, 29–30). By 2016, trust in government remained quite low and popular discontent quite high. The political outsider Donald Trump, with no governmental experience but great personal wealth and a vivid media profile, could echo these views effectively—and did. His "drain the swamp" mantra was effective political shorthand that both diagnosed the problem and pointed toward a solution.

Providing a workable solution would prove harder for Trump than he ever acknowledged on the campaign stump. He took office during what political scientist Byron Shafer calls an "era of political volatility," begun during Bill Clinton's presidency, featuring a wide range of electoral outcomes, a "kaleidoscope" of "limitless electoral possibilities in very short order" (Shafer 2016, 123). Trump is the latest electoral surprise in this sequence, following the partisan zigzag of the Clinton, George W. Bush, and Obama presidencies, featuring Republican, Democratic, and divided partisan Congresses.

The era of political volatility has four major traits. The first is a close national partisan balance between the two major parties. The rise of Republican dominance in the conservative but previously Democratic South and of Democratic dominance in the more liberal and previously electorally competitive Northeast helped to produce a "growing ideological polarization in multiple issue domains that are nevertheless increasingly aligned" that "represented nothing less than a blanketing nationalization of American party politics" (Shafer 2016, 149). The second trait of ideological polarization between the parties received reinforcement by the rising dominance of ideological activists in the parties: "The ideological dynamic that has captured the activist stratum" eventually captured "elected officialdom" and fostered "generalized polarization" (Shafer 2016, 141).

Ideological politics produced a third trait, in which all issue conflicts gradually lined up along the partisan, ideological divide: "All the great policy domains of the modern world—economic welfare, foreign affairs, civil rights, and cultural values—collapsed into one dimension, liberals versus conservatives by way of Democrats versus Republicans" (Shafer 2016, 191). When all issues are fought on one partisan front, governmental stagnation will frequently occur when partisan control of government is divided between the parties, as it was in 1995–2001, 2007–2009, and 2013–2017. National policymaking was "characterized by long stretches of intense partisan warfare, interrupted only intermittently by spikes of legislative activity, the product of which was often omnibus legislation, bundling a set of major concerns that could relieve the pressure for action while allocating rewards on all sides" (Shafer 2016, 167). Major partisan legislative breakthroughs included Bill Clinton's economic stimulus bill of 1993, George W. Bush's tax cuts of 2001, and Barack Obama's economic stimulus in 2009 and Affordable Care Act in 2010. Examples of bipartisan omnibus legislative breakthroughs included a budget deal in 1995, a tax cut in 2011, and fiscal legislation to reopen the government in 2013.

Into this environment walked President Donald Trump. Before we undertake a detailed inventory of his prospects, it's worth noting some immediate consequences for Trump from the three defining characteristics of his "political time" that we have just sketched. Wage stagnation and trade and automation-based job losses were highlighted by candidate Trump, so improvement on those fronts is essential to his successful presidency. Quick improvement on such long-standing problems, however, will be difficult to deliver. Though Trump, the outsider candidate, capitalized on distrust of government and popular discontent during the 2016 campaign, as president these features of public opinion may prove inimical to his success. A "kaleidoscopic" national political order where anything is possible portends great uncertainties for his presidency. Things can go well or poorly in very short order. Trump is not the beneficiary of a durable electoral coalition or a securely dominant political party.

DONALD TRUMP'S POLITICAL CAPITAL

We have introduced the general term "political capital" in previous chapters. Here we explore the concepts more thoroughly in order to assess Donald Trump's political prospects in the White House. The concept involves several important indicators of presidential governance and public support: presidential job approval, support for the president's party, and congressional support for the president. An additional measure involves the number of executive branch appointments available to the president. A better indicator of "appointment capital" for Trump in his early presidency is how many appointments he has made and have been confirmed by the Senate. The president's early appointment record reveals how well he is using this capital asset at the outset of his administration.

A president with high political capital will enjoy job approval from popular majorities, head a political party enjoying more favorable opinion from the public than its major party rival, and receive high levels of success with his legislation on the House and Senate floors. In addition, high political capital is evident in a large number of successful executive branch appointments early in a president's administration. How does Trump stack up in these regards?

Useful indexes of public approval of a president's job performance, updated daily, appear on statistical guru Nate Silver's website FiveThirtyEight. There, almost all publicly released polls of presidential job approval are folded into an index of job approval. Website analysts weight a poll's contribution to the index based on the poll's "methodological standards" and historical accuracy (Silver 2017). Three daily approval/disapproval averages appear of all polls, polls of likely and registered voters, and polls of all adults.

Trump's public approval trends since his inauguration are exceptional. No president since presidential approval surveys began in the middle 1930s has had such low approval and high disapproval in the first eight months in office. On January 20, Trump's approval average for all polls was 45.5 percent, for surveys of all adults 45 percent, and for polls of likely and registered voters only 41 percent. This proved to be Trump's "high-water mark" in polling thus far in his first term. By March 17, popular majorities in all surveys and surveys of adults disapproved of his job performance, and two days later majorities in polls of registered and likely voters expressed disapproval. Since then, Trump's job approval has been "majority negative" on all three poll indexes, with his job approval gradually slipping from the mid-forties to slightly below 40 percent ("How Popular Is Donald Trump?" 2017).

Trump's unprecedented early unpopularity stemmed from his stunning election victory despite losing the popular vote and his contentious behavior as both candidate and president. No president upon winning an election has faced such vociferous "resistance" by hostile interests and elected officials. The "resisters" employed an extraordinary range of oppositional tactics. Efforts were undertaken to encourage presidential electors to switch their votes away from Trump, force recounts in closely contested states, boycott the Inauguration, block or delay presidential appointments, leak unflattering information about Trump, sue to remove the president under the emoluments clause of the Constitution, declare Trump unfit for office under the Twenty-fifth Amendment, judicially block executive orders, and promise impending impeachment.

The intensity fueling such tactics was reflected in surveys revealing that those who "strongly disapprove" of his job performance by the president's first summer in office stood at more than 40 percent and almost double the percentage "strongly approving" of the president (Salant 2017). In polling, Trump's political capital stands at an unprecedented low. Sixty-five percent of those disapproving his job performance in a July 2017 Gallup poll cited Trump's personality as the reason for their disapprobation (Newport 2017). It may be difficult for the president to overcome widespread dislike for him as a person. The president himself reportedly accepts that he will never be broadly popular and thus concentrates his policies and communications on his "base" of 2016 supporters (Allen 2017).

Trump's election did not produce a popular surge in favorable views of the Republican Party. The nonpartisan Pew Center has found that favorable views of the GOP have lagged behind those of Democrats since 2010, with GOP favorable averaging just below 40 percent during that time. In June 2017, 40 percent of adults had a favorable view of the Republicans while 44 percent had positive views of the Democratic Party. Fifty-four percent found the GOP "too extreme," but only 45 percent so described Democrats. Polarization had grown since January, with increasing percentages of Republicans and Democrats adopting negative views of the rival party (Pew Research Center 2017).

Initial congressional support for Trump's legislative agenda has not been resounding. In his administration's first six months, more than forty bills passed and gained the president's signature, a historically high number. Most of those, however, involved regulatory rollbacks under the Congressional Review Act. His one important policy achievement came on June 23 when he signed a law creating a new policy protecting whistleblowers in the Department of Veterans Affairs (Hansler 2017). Sixty percent of the bills Trump has signed are one page long (Bump 2017). Trump scored a major success in the appointment of Neil Gorsuch to the Supreme Court, but he lags in his number of submitted judicial nominees and administration appointments. Senate Democrats have contributed to the appointment backlog by slowing the appointment process in the Senate.

Many major legislative agenda items had yet to make their way through Congress by 2017's summer. Repealing and replacing Obama's Affordable Care Act, having passed the House by only a two-vote margin, remained stalled in the Senate. Major tax reform has yet to emerge from any legislative committee. Trump's plans for big infrastructure spending have not yet resulted in an administration proposal to Congress. The House and Senate by August had yet to act on an increase in the federal debt limit or budget for the next fiscal year. A generous grade for Trump with Congress is "incomplete"—evidence of substantial political capital there has yet to appear.

The appointments backlog is another political capital problem for Trump. His administration has been slow to nominate and Congress slow to approve his appointees, resulting in many executive branch positions staffed by holdover appointees from the previous administration or career bureaucrats. "Decisions don't get made as well, as quickly or as effectively without a presidentially appointed, Senate-confirmed, person in place," according to Max Stier of the Partnership for Public Service, which tracks administration nominations (Pramuk 2017).

Trump's presidential success ultimately derives from his levels of political capital. As we wrote in an earlier book, "The decline in political capital has produced great difficulties for presidential leadership in recent decades. It is difficult to claim warrants for leadership in an era when job approval, congressional support, and partisan affiliation provide less backing for a president than in times past. Because of the uncertainties of political capital, recent presidents have adopted a governing style that is personalized, preemptive and, at times, isolated" (Schier and Eberly 2013, 95).

Trump's style is personalized, preemptive, and at times isolated. He continues to present the outsized media persona that characterized his business career and his presidential campaign. Trump's tweets certainly are highly personalized. A "preemptive" president "is not out to establish, uphold or salvage any political orthodoxy. Theirs is an unabashedly mongrel politics; it is an aggressive critique of the prevailing political categories" (Skowronek 1997, 449). Preemptive presidents included Richard Nixon, Woodrow Wilson, and Bill Clinton, each trying to chart his own way without careful observance of previous political orthodoxies. Nixon proved less conservative than previous GOP presidents, Clinton more centrist, and Wilson more progressive than previous Democrats. Each encountered serious political challenges—impeachment charges brought against Clinton, invalidism born of political defeat for Wilson, and probable impeachment and resignation for Nixon.

Trump's political career is one of a preemptive outsider. His policies on infrastructure, foreign policy, trade, and immigration have proven divisive and controversial within his own party. Rival Democrats recoil from his original political approach. He clearly seeks to rearrange preexisting political categories. Preemptive presidents tend to arouse opposition from those attached to previous political ideologies and alignments. It is a dangerous presidential path.

One clear and present danger for the president is a difficult media environment, one he helped to create and probably cannot escape. The president early in his term expressed surprise at the strongly negative media coverage he continues to receive. He remains the target of anonymous leaks, many of them of dubious accuracy, seized upon by reporters. Many in the bureaucracies and organizations of "permanent Washington" plant such stories in order to impede Trump's presidency. Trump invited such treatment with his fiery condemnation of conventional Washington politics both as a candidate and in office. His controversial and at times peculiar and inaccurate tweets do little to burnish his credibility with a skeptical media or with many in the public beyond his minority base of supporters. Once the media fixes on a hostile narrative—in this case, the story of the uncouth and unqualified President Trump—it's difficult for any president to escape the problem. The persistence of the "Trump-Russia collusion" story, despite no major evidence in its support, is an example of Trump's media predicament.

Donald Trump's initial political capital in the White House has proven to be unusually low. Add to that Trump's flamboyant and contentious presidential style, a difficult relationship with the media, and the result is an extraordinary White House denizen who is tempting political fate. The unusual politics of a preemptive president invite few reliable allies over time. Political isolation can result, portending big trouble for the president's party. That is one possibility for Trump's presidential future, one of several we next explore.

Triumphant Trump?

It's possible that Donald Trump will rise from his administration's inauspicious beginnings to become a successful president and a dominant political force. A string of major policy successes along with changes in the president's behavior would be necessary for his political rebound. Legislatively, this means passage and popularity of the American Health Care Act, the GOP replacement of Obama's Affordable Care Act. Congress also then passes an extension of the debt ceiling, a fiscal year 2018 budget, tax cuts and tax reform, and a large spending bill to improve the nation's infrastructure—all acceptable to and celebrated by the White House and large segments of the public. Trump's administration increases its pace of judicial and administrative appointments, and these appointments receive quicker congressional approval. In foreign policy, Trump's trade policies produce better deals for the United States, ISIS suffers conclusive defeat, and the threat of international terrorism abates. Trump also finds a way to contain North Korea short of regional war.

The president improves his Twitter strategy, resulting in better media coverage. The avalanche of anonymous, damaging leaks abates as he enjoys policy successes. Trump's popularity with political independents grows, and for the first time in his presidency he enjoys majority public approval. Republicans hold Congress in the 2018 midterms, and Trump arrives at 2020 in a strong position for reelection.

This may seem fanciful, but many of the above events are within the realm of possibility. Trump might improve his public standing by following the advice of media veteran Bill O'Reilly: "Tweet facts, Mr. President, not insults. Hammer your opposition with verifiable statements" (O'Reilly 2017). His ideological position with the public includes potential for the growth in public approval. Law professor F. H. Buckley, drawing on an extensive survey of public opinion assembled by the nonpartisan Voter Survey Group, argues that Trump occupies the "sweet spot" of American politics: "The sweet spot in American politics, the place where elections are won, is the socially conservative and economically liberal quadrant. And the winner is going to be the fellow who's not going to touch Social Security and who promises to nominate a judge in the mold of Antonin Scalia. Donald Trump, in other words" (Buckley 2017). To Buckley, the Democratic Party's dedication to liberal "identity politics" will prevent it from winning the support of vital, socially conservative voters. Trump, he argues, has a big advantage with them.

If Trump manages to rack up a string of congressional and foreign policy successes, change his tweet strategy, and improve his media treatment and his White House management, he can dominate US politics. This seems a long shot, because of Trump's preemptive, seemingly unchangeable, and contentious political style. He remains a stranger to many GOP policymakers, an enemy to many in the media, and is anathema to practically all Democrats. His inexperience in office may well prevent the successes his presidency so sorely needs in legislation and foreign affairs. But with a few breaks, more competence, better manners, and maintenance of his "sweet spot," a much brighter future might be his.

Decline and Fall?

This worst-case scenario begins with Special Counsel Robert Mueller recommending criminal charges against several members of the Trump campaign and administration for illegalities in their relationship with the Russian government. A deluge of negative media coverage ensues. Trump, though not charged, faces cries for his resignation. Though the GOP Congress refuses to act on impeachment charges drawn up by Democrats, a "wave" election in 2018 produces Democratic majorities in the US House and Senate. The House majority votes approval of several articles of impeachment, and the Senate either removes Trump from office with 67 Democratic votes or fails to convict.

If he survives a Senate impeachment trial, Trump then limps through the remainder of his term as a greatly damaged president, unable to effectively direct domestic or foreign policy. Though his tweets remain as tart as ever, his sympathetic audience shrinks far below his 2016 popular base. Media coverage remains overwhelmingly negative. The 2020 election proves disastrous for the GOP, whether or not Trump decides to run for reelection. Along the way, foreign policy reversals on trade, North Korea, and the Middle East worsen Trump's political standing.

By July 2017, 25 Democrats had agreed to sponsor an impeachment resolution against Donald Trump. Absent Mueller's findings, their bill proposes setting up a congressional "oversight" commission that could declare the president incapacitated, leading to his removal from office, due to personal incapacity, under the Twenty-fifth Amendment to the US Constitution (Bowden 2017). Democrats are also pursuing a lawsuit arguing that Trump violated the emoluments clause of the Constitution due to the foreign investments of his enterprises. Adverse findings from Mueller will certainly enhance impeachment-related activity.

Public opinion on impeachment is potentially ominous for Trump. Surveys in summer 2017 indicated that at least 40 percent of US adults favored some form of impeachment proceedings against the president. Previous presidents George W. Bush and Bill Clinton also incurred pro-impeachment sentiments of more than 30 percent in polls. Trump's high numbers reflect his provocative personality and the greater partisan polarization of the country. Large majorities of Democrats want impeachment proceedings to begin, but less than a majority of Independents agree, and very few Republicans are on board with impeachment (Brewster 2017).

So "many shoes have to drop" before Trump experiences a fall from office during his first term. His preemptive presidency, volatile personality, negative media coverage, and a deeply polarized nation brimming with partisan "resistance" make this a greater possibility than any president since Bill Clinton has experienced. Yet in his first year in office, few (if any) of the conditions for his removal from the presidency are in place.

More of the Same?

Continuity is often a safe bet in life and in politics. What might produce a future trajectory for Trump similar to that of his first six months in office? First, Trump's base, the focus of much of his presidential persuasion, would have to stick with him. Since the president's sweeping campaign promises on immigration, economics, and trade are not very likely to become reality, "Trump nation" will have to demonstrate considerable patience as his term transpires.

Second, Democrats would continue to oppose and obstruct the president in Congress and in elections. That is certainly a safe bet, given the activities of the "resistance" since Election Day 2016. Democrats may have learned, however, that simply being anti-Trump is not a winning formula. That message did not help them win any of the four congressional by-elections during Trump's initial months in office. Their new 2018 campaign slogan—"A Better Deal"—seeks to beat the presidential deal maker at his own game.

Anonymous leaks and continuous stories about a quirky and peculiar Trump would continue to dominate the media. Over time, however, the effect of the media coverage changes fewer minds among the public. In a polarized America, many citizens choose media sources reflecting their partisan and ideological biases. After several months, media coverage serves to merely reinforce existing public divisions about Trump. The "news" about Trump doesn't get better or worse in its content or political effect.

"More of the same" requires Republicans to retain control of Congress while Trump's fellow partisans in the legislature work fitfully with a mercurial and inexperienced chief executive. The 2020 presidential election—with or without Trump—proves competitive. A wounded GOP candidate faces off against a decidedly liberal Democratic rival with the outcome very much in doubt.

How does the country fare with more of the same? The economy grows slowly but perhaps steadily, little progress is made containing the North Korean threat, deficits continue as the public debt grows. National health care policy remains replete with problems as Medicaid and Medicare costs inexorably rise. The nation's infrastructure continues to be very much in need of repair. ISIS recedes, but US involvement in the Middle East does not. Environmental policy remains in reverse from the Obama years. National tax reform remains an aspiration. The cultural civil war between identity politics liberals and social conservatives rages on.

Meanwhile, America remains acutely divided between liberals and conservatives, Republicans and Democrats. The divisions ensure stasis, more of the same. Popular discontent and low trust in government persist as they have since the 1960s. Donald Trump, the incendiary president, frequently fuels the conflicts but maintains a cantankerous course that fails to improve the prospects for his presidency or the nation.

So, Overall . . .

For all the sound and fury of the Trump presidency, The Donald's time at 1600 Pennsylvania Avenue seems unlikely to reshape the three defining traits of our present political era. Recalling Byron Shafer's analysis, Trump is the personification of an "era of political volatility," and his controversial persona seems likely to maintain a "long stretch of intense partisan warfare" during his presidency. Many of his reversals of Obama's unilateral executive actions can be quickly overturned by a rival successor in the White House. Trump's unpopularity and negative media coverage, however, may alter the "close partisan balance" that Shafer notes characterizes our political present, to the detriment of the Republican Party.

Rising economic inequality, the loss of manufacturing jobs, and slow economic growth have plagued the nation's economy for decades, and it's unlikely that any Trump administration policies will reverse those trends in the short term—even if they pass Congress, which is far from certain. Popular discontent and low trust in government, festering since the 1960s, helped elect Trump. His ongoing criticisms of establishment Washington help to maintain that low trust and discontent. Foreign policy remains his greatest opportunity for a lasting legacy, for good or ill.

Donald Trump's highly unorthodox presidency features extraordinary levels of verbal swordplay, much generated by the president himself. The cumulative result of all the querulous verbiage may be remarkably modest. Consider this saying attributed to Mark Twain: "Action speaks louder than words but not nearly as often" (*Los Angeles Times* 2010).

WORKS CITED

Alden, Edward. *Failure to Adjust: How Americans Got Left Behind the Global Economy*. Lanham, MD: Rowman & Littlefield, 2017.

Allen, Mike. "Trump's Inner Bannon." *Axios AM*. July 5, 2017. https://www.axios.com/axios-am 2453605865.html?utm_source=newsletter&utm_medium=email&utm_campaign=newsletter_axiosam&stream=top-stories (accessed July 11, 2017).

Bowden, John. "More Dems Sign On to Bill to Impeach Trump." *The Hill*. July 1, 2017. http://thehill.com/homenews/administration/340392-more-dems-sign-onto-bill-to-impeach-trump (accessed July 11, 2017).

Brewster, Jack. "Why You Should Be Skeptical About Polls on Impeaching Trump." *Time*. June 7, 2017. http://time.com/4808071/donald-trump-impeachment-polls/ (accessed July 11, 2017).

Buckley, F. H. "Trump's Still Sitting in the Sweet Spot of American Politics." *New York Post*. June 29, 2017. http://nypost.com/2017/06/29/trumps-still -sitting-in-the-sweet-spot-of-american-politics/ (accessed July 11, 2017).

Bump, Phillip. "60 Percent of the Bills Trump Has Signed into Law Are One Page Long." *Washington Post*. July 5, 2017. https://www.washingtonpost.com/ news/politics/wp/2017/07/05/60-percent-of-the-bills-trump-has-signed-into -law-have-been-one-page-long/?utm_term=.f8cdccbf71be (accessed July 11, 2017).

Bureau of Labor Statistics. "Table B-1: Employees on Nonfarm Payrolls." February 5, 2017. https://www.bls.gov/webapps/legacy/cesbtab1.htm (accessed July 11, 2017).

Desilver, Drew. "The Many Ways to Measure Economic Inequality." Pew Research Center. September 22, 2015. http://www.pewresearch.org/fact-tank/2015/09/22/ the-many-ways-to-measure-economic-inequality/ (accessed July 11, 2017).

Federal Reserve Board. "Survey of Consumer Finances." July 11, 2013. https:// www.federalreserve.gov/econres/scfindex.htm (accessed July 11, 2017).

Fry, Richard, and Rakesh Kochhar. "America's Wealth Gap between Middle-Income and Upper-Income Families Is Widest on Record." Pew Research Center. December 17, 2014. http://www.pewresearch.org/fact-tank/2014/12/17/ wealth-gap-upper-middle-income/ (accessed July 11, 2017).

Hansler, Jennifer. "President Trump Has Signed 40 Bills into Law. Here's What They Do." CNN. June 29, 2017. http://www.cnn.com/2017/06/29/politics/president -trump-legislation/index.html (accessed July 11, 2017).

"How Popular Is Donald Trump?" FiveThirtyEight. August 10, 2017. https:// fivethirtyeight.com/ (accessed August 10, 2017).

Los Angeles Times. "Top of the Ticket: 100 Years Ago Today Reports of Mark Twain's Death Were No Longer Greatly Exaggerated." April 21, 2010. http:// latimesblogs.latimes.com/washington/2010/04/samuel-clemens-mark-twain .html (accessed July 24, 2017).

Luhby, Tami. "The Middle Class Gets a Big Raise . . . Finally." CNN Money. September 13, 2016. http://money.cnn.com/2016/09/13/news/economy/median -income-census/index.html (accessed July 11, 2017).

Newport, Frank. "Trump Disapproval Rooted in Character Concerns." *Gallup*. July 13, 2017. http://www.gallup.com/poll/214091/trump-disapproval-rooted -character-concerns.aspx (accessed August 21, 2017).

Nye, Joseph S., Jr., and Phillip E. Zelikow. "Conclusions: Reflections, Conjectures and Puzzles." In Joseph S. Nye Jr., Phillip E. Zelikow, and David C. King, eds., *Why People Don't Trust Government*. Cambridge, MA: Harvard University Press, 1997.

O'Reilly, Bill. "How Trump Will Win His War against the Media." *The Hill*. July 5, 2017. http://thehill.com/blogs/pundits-blog/media/340643-opinion-how -trump-will-win-his-war-against-the-media (accessed July 11, 2017).

Pew Research Center. "Public Has Criticisms of Both Parties, but Democrats Lead on Empathy for Middle Class." June 20, 2017. http://www.people-press .org/2017/06/20/public-has-criticisms-of-both-parties-but-democrats-lead-on -empathy-for-middle-class/ (accessed July 11, 2017).

Pramuk, Jacob. "Trump Is Having a Hard Time Hiring People—And Constant Turmoil Doesn't Help." CNBC. May 29, 2017. http://www.cnbc.com/2017/05/31/ trump-has-a-hiring-problem-and-white-house-turmoil-isnt-helping.html (accessed July 11, 2017).

Salant, Jonathan D. "2 New Polls Reveal What Americans Think of Trump." NJ.com. June 30, 2017. http://www.nj.com/politics/index.ssf/2017/06/what_ americans_now_think_of_president_trump.html (accessed July 11, 2017).

Schier, Steven E., and Todd E. Eberly. *American Government and Popular Discontent: Stability without Success*. New York: Routledge, 2013.

Schier, Steven E., and Todd E. Eberly. *Polarized: The Rise of Ideology in American Politics*. Lanham, MD: Rowman & Littlefield, 2016.

Shafer, Byron E. *The American Political Pattern*. Lawrence: University Press of Kansas, 2016.

Silver, Nate. "How We're Tracking Donald Trump's Approval Ratings." FiveThirtyEight. March 2, 2017. http://fivethirtyeight.com/features/how-were -tracking-donald-trumps-approval-ratings/ (accessed July 11, 2017).

Skowronek, Stephen. *The Politics Presidents Make: Leadership from John Adams to Bill Clinton*. Cambridge, MA: Harvard University Press, 1997.

Index